Inbox Full

Based on a true story

ISBN-13:978-1456548810

ISBN-10:1456548816

Cover: Michael Woestehoff

To my beautiful daughters,

with love and gratitude for everything you both are, and to my parents,

family and friends all over the world – thank you for sharing this journey.

Inbox Full

I read today that you can describe a woman by the contents of her handbag. Whilst you can't judge a book by its cover, you can understand many secrets of a woman by peering in her handbag. I've never minded anyone looking in mine...

One British passport (just in case) and five old boarding passes ranging from Sleazy Jet to Nice, to Virgin upper class to NYC.

Two toothbrushes and paste (BA business class).

Marlboro Lights, two broken lighters, and matches from places I don't remember going.

One beautiful faux leopard skin purse bursting with three inches of receipts I keep for no reason (including black cabs, the cost of which make me feel sick).

Half a dozen credit cards unused for years (no credit available).

Enough euros, Thai baht, U.S. and Barbados dollars to get a taxi, pay for a drink and make a call from anywhere in the world if I found myself stranded without a signal.

Stacks of business cards from people I have no reason or interest to call.

Two unpaid parking tickets courtesy of Chelsea and Westminster Council London, the fine rising like a soufflé, bastards.

A dozen children's hair clips and elastics, belonging to my daughters Daisy and Amber.

My phone

Three sets of keys, two of which no longer work, and one set of keys to a testament of German engineering (partially paid off) in the form of a big black gas guzzler otherwise known as a Chelsea tractor but unlike the type you watch with embarrassment trying to park outside Peter Jones on the King's Road, I actually needed it for work! I loved it. It had a killer sound system too.

Another set of keys, which should have been to my own castle, but these in fact opened the door to someone else's dream that I was paying through the nose to rent!

A small blue book called 'The Journey From Lost to Found,' *by Susan Jeffers.*

MAY 7, 2004

The beginning of the end

Outbox	Olivier
Olivier?	Oui, Si, Ja, Yes?
Options Reply Open	Options Reply Open

Outbox	Olivier
Do you remember me? We met in London 5 months ago! You asked me to have dinner with you...	Of course I do with all your friends on the Kings Road. It would be my pleasure. Tues in London? Thurs in Paris? Or Barcelona Fri?
Options Reply Open	Options Reply Open

We did all three...

MAY 18TH, 2004—ELEVEN DAYS LATER

I knew I'd crossed the line when I pressed that button and sent the first text to Olivier but I had gone and done it, eyes wide open, there was no turning back, no rewinding the clock. Like sand through my fingers the desire to be with my husband had just slipped away over the last few months, and now, here I am standing almost numb, surveying the grand hallway of the house on Menorca, the tiny island off the coast of Spain where my husband Tom and I live with our two little girls, piled ceiling-high with boxes, unable to think straight. I am supposed to be here unpacking our life in our incredible manor house in the Mediterranean—our new 'family' home.

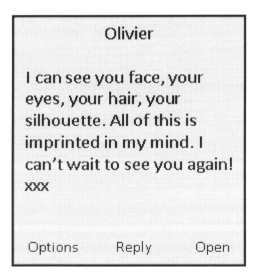

Olivier

I can see you face, your eyes, your hair, your silhouette. All of this is imprinted in my mind. I can't wait to see you again! xxx

Options   Reply   Open

I feel like I am losing my mind, entering a nightmare that only I have orchestrated. I had a husband who supposedly loved me, or at least he thought he did, even though I was often referred to as his trophy wife.

How could I break his heart? If I chose now I could lose everything I cherished, everything we'd worked for.

Two years ago we had escaped the English countryside and the rain, leaving all the middle-aged, green-wellied bores behind, who did nothing but talk ponies and school fees. No social climbing bullshit or wanker banker chat in sight. I was desperate to get him off the phone permanently attached to his ear, free him from his eternal stress, endless staff and responsibilities and remember what really mattered. The opposite in fact. Our life in Spain was going to be nirvana, where we were going to flourish, enjoy the happiness of watching our girls grow up. Where we were going to live in bikinis and shorts, sit in the sun, eat gambas, all the vegetables from our garden, drink wine and live happily ever after.

And when we heard about this house, Bona Ventura (meaning good luck), we had been so impatient to see it we scrambled over the high walls, overgrown with blackberries, to take it all in before being shown around. It is a beautiful, unique 17th-century manor house. Even through its disrepair, its lack of love and a mountain of cash the size of Kilimanjaro needed to create it, we could see the vision. It is everything we had dreamt of. I truly loved this place.

The approach is a mile-long straight drive leading up to this Palladian style home, with symmetrical steps rising up to the original entrance. Below hang the ancient arched wooden doors where the horse and cart would have entered in years gone by. Massive stone vaulted rooms, extensive attics crying out to be made into heavenly bedrooms, and wild formal gardens and pathways blanketed in bougainvillea. It has a large summer house, replicating the main house with a labyrinth maze, surrounded by orchards with apples, mulberries and melons with dozens of types of fruit and vegetables. It is in the middle of nowhere set against the backdrop of miles of pinewoods with the blue Mediterranean beyond. There are no electrics, just a generator, and water is provided by the old well. No post. No rubbish collection. No neighbors. No parking wardens. You are on your own out here, miles from the nearest town.

I'd imagined everything we have here together to be my idea of heaven. Creating this house into our dream was the most exciting project of our lives. I had thought this would bring us back together, unite us and restore the magic that Tom and I had lost over the past two years.

But none of that was going to happen now. Nothing could ever be the same again. Not after what I'd got myself into. With tickets paid for, waiting for me, I'd flown off the island three times in the last eleven days to rendezvous around Europe with Olivier. I had consciously, singlehandedly just shattered all we had here into a thousand pieces.

I needed my best friend Jules but couldn't reach her so I texted her:

I had every emotion known to mankind going through me. I hadn't had peace day or night for weeks; I could barely sleep at all. Within minutes, her answer came through:

Jules

Well sweetheart look on
the bright side....
At least you will only have
to pack half that stuff up!
xxx

Options   Reply   Open

I pulled the cork on a cold bottle of wine just as she rang. Thank god, I was desperate

to speak to her. She always found something positive to say, however inappropriate. We

both burst into laughter at her text in a strange, nervous way, immediately followed by

heavy sighs. Neither of us, in our decades of friendship and experiences, had ever been

here before. It was terrifying, like holding a national secret between us. The weight of the

seriousness and danger of it was very clear.

> ## Olivier
>
> I keep trying to imagine you in your wonderful home I hope we can create a home as beautiful as that together one day xxx
>
> Options   Reply   Open

My heart full, I took my wine and left the unpacked boxes to go and sit down on the old stone steps in the sun's warmth with the dogs at my feet. Not a person or a building in sight, just fields of flowers, and silence. I watched the long grass swaying in the evening breeze like a calming swell. I closed my eyes and took a deep breath, praying for courage and strength; I was going to need every bit I could find.

It was too late. My marriage was over and Jules and I were the only two people in the world that knew. In nine years of being with Tom I had never swapped a number, stolen a kiss or ever even contemplated an affair. But Tom's irregular trips back to the UK for work had begun to be the weekly routine, which was never the plan, leaving me for longer periods of time alone with no friends, no social life and my only company being our au pair, a chain-smoking Croatian tiger. I was not a woman who ever wanted to be left at home, but I found myself left on the island increasingly lonely and unfulfilled. Within the confines of the blue-washed walls I was turning into a pacing lioness eying up the lovely tiger as my only prey.

There were no neighbors for miles most of the year round; in fact our first home in Menorca, Casa San Francisco, was in such a remote spot that even the street lights were turned off six months of the year. The town went from being a buzzing summer retreat with a constant flow of guests to a deathly dark, deserted scene, like something out of 'Butch Cassidy and the Sundance Kid' where the Tramontana wind could blow for days at a time.

Menorca translates as 'island of change,' and there were more suicides from the effects of the relentless high winds than anything else in the Balearics. I used to joke about one day being found hanging from our enormous palm tree, hopefully wearing a killer pair of heels that I never got to wear anymore.

Last December I was climbing the walls dying to be with people who knew me back home. I wanted to speak my own language, eat at one of my favorite places, let my hair down and generally be with my soul mates; be me. I was well overdue a respite from solitude.

Finally, I was given the green light to get away, so I headed for the UK and left the girls for the weekend with Tom and his parents. Though we had lived in Spain for the past two years, at the top of my wish list that year was a pre-Christmas dinner with my best friends in London—it was all I wanted. I had arranged to meet the gang for dinner on the King's Road in Chelsea at the restaurant 'Eight over Eight.' I headed straight there from the airport after a quick shower at Jules's house in Fulham.

I burst in that door like a steam train headed off the rails and found myself staring straight into a face I wasn't looking for. Who the hell was he? These eyes burnt through me with such intensity for a split second I forgot what I was doing, who I was meeting or in fact even who I was! After the whirlwind of hugs and greetings to all my favorite people I turned to find those eyes again. I couldn't help myself. He was standing listening to his friend talking to him in French at five thousand miles an hour. He wasn't paying any attention. He was looking right at me.

I looked away. No one had ever looked at me in that way before, No one. As his group went to their table, he paused, and murmured, "You seem to have a lot of friends here tonight. I am lucky to be able to get a table, I see." His accent was so delicious you could have melted chocolate with it and his smile literally made my knees buckle. The last time I felt like that I was standing in a phone booth during the San Francisco earthquake in 1989.

All through dinner I had no appetite and even the hilarious conversations around me seemed a blur as I tried not to look over at him looking at me. He was breathtakingly beautiful. When he introduced himself and gave me his card as he left, I took it and I gave him mine.

Within minutes he called me. "Would you consider having dinner with me one day?" As much as I was dying to say "Yes!" this other voice inside me just took over on the phone, like an operator interrupting a call.

"That's sweet of you to ask," I replied. "I'd have loved to in another life. It was a pleasure to meet you." Ten minutes later, he tried again.

"No, thank you," I said, my voice shaking. "Please don't call me again. I can NEVER do that... Goodbye."

He rang again, I didn't answer. And then again, so I turned my phone off, sick to my stomach at how alive I felt. I wanted to pretend that none of it had ever happened. That I hadn't just given my number to a beautiful stranger, though he was all I could think of which was madness.I was desperate to avoid the fact that I had opened my mind and now something inside me had changed forever. I returned home to the island and tried to get back to my normal life. My husband, my babies, and my home were waiting for me, so like an Oscar-winning performer I played my role, loathing myself, every second of every day.

For the next four long months my husband and I worked flat out with a team of eleven from all over the world to make the main bedrooms and bathrooms livable so that we could move in. I should have been dizzy with excitement. The problem was there was only one thing consuming me and it wouldn't go away. In the beginning every time the vision of Olivier and that dinner in London popped in I had pushed it to the darkest corner of my mind. He was a Swiss banker, married with two daughters and living in Geneva.

But my world had been turned upside down and inside out. Gradually over the weeks, thoughts of him started coming in again, uninvited, completely throwing me off course. I could have been doing anything from choosing wallpaper to deciding how many types of cheese I was buying, and suddenly there he was, even though he lived in another country with another wife and his own happy family.

I couldn't escape the thought of him, no matter where I was. I felt myself shutting down on my husband, detaching from him even more, and hating myself for realizing I was thinking about somebody else. Someone else's husband.

Worried friends talked to Tom, warning him to pay attention. I was miserable and it was written all over my face, visible to everyone other than him. He always told them I'd never leave and if I did, I'd be lost without him. The picture of my blissful marriage was all an illusion. There was no denying it anymore. We may as well have been strangers. I didn't feel loved. I didn't feel appreciated. I didn't feel desirable at all anymore. Throughout that entire spring I was lost. I found it impossible to connect with him, as we seemed to be only passing ships in the night. The longer it went on, the harder it was to feel anything. All I saw between Tom and me was sad empty space.

Then one day, I was hanging out the washing when I just sat down and stared at my phone. What if I called Olivier? Or, I thought, what if I just texted him? I fiddled around writing brief messages in a confused state, and then deleted them straight away, again and again. For weeks I'd do the same thing—write messages and delete them- getting so close I'd even pull the car over to just sit there, my thumb on the send button. I'd stare down at the phone. Then I'd return to the house with a bootload of plants or color samples for me to experiment with and try to get on with the rest of my life.

But one day as I walked the long drive in the midday sun, I couldn't resist my thumb or that button anymore. And I did it. I sent the first message. The one that changed my entire destiny, forever.

> **Olivier**
>
> I can't believe that I'm not going to see you tonight. I feel like I'm walking to the edge of a cliff and that I'm going to fall into the emptiness... xxx
>
> Options   Reply   Open

After seeing Olivier again after all these months, I could not delay any longer telling Tom I wanted to separate. I sat him down when he arrived back on the island under our palm tree and delivered the painful blow, which I'd been dreading.

I told him how deeply unhappy I had become. I blamed myself, and hugely regretted not communicating enough over the years. I had pretended to be stronger than I was. I should have made it clearer to him that I had needed more of his time, his attention, respect and love. Not material things. He had spent even more time away from me, arriving back every week even more exhausted, even more stressed out than he was in the UK and our plan hadn't worked out. He had continued to take me for granted and we were both responsible for losing our way.

I had no idea what was going to happen in the future but I couldn't play this role any longer. I couldn't keep pretending our marriage was fine, when it was everything but. I said that I needed to separate, not divorce, as that was too final and too hasty.

I didn't tell him about Olivier, as I knew he would just blame that. I knew in my own heart that I had thought about another man for five months that I had met for a mere five minutes, but I needed this separation even without Olivier in the picture. It was the hardest thing I had ever done getting those words finally out. He was absolutely furious. He told me I was insane. I was wrong. Nothing I wasn't expecting but the whole conversation was obviously hideously painful, full stop.

This diary has been staring at me from the top shelf in the kitchen collecting dust, beckoning me since I was given it about two months ago. It has sat in various places around the house crying out to be written in. I'd open it up frequently, thumb my way through the clean paper, then put it safely back but last I've picked it up and written the first paragraph on this very bank page staring at me. (A gift from my special friend Laura, who along with this, gave me a candle to remind me of my inner light, and worry people from South America in a tiny silk pouch to share my thoughts with before putting them under my pillow at night.)

Why has it taken all this time to start writing? Did I not know where to start? Or was it the fact I was scared of finding a secret place to keep it along with all my thoughts at the age of thirty-three? I know the excuse to myself was never being able to find a decent pen, but the real truth is I was afraid of what I'd end up writing about, the fact it would show me in black and white where my life was headed right now.

Well here I go … My head is filled with so many emotions right now I don't know which I feel more of, regret, pain, helplessness, guilt, sadness, confusion, love, loss, shock, panic, FEAR? How the hell did I get here?

What has changed in me to feel like I've got to here, yet I'm empty, hollow, unfulfilled. Is this just the beginning for me? Why have I turned a corner now? Why can't I just get on with my 'blissful life'? If I love it all then what am I missing out on? What exactly am I looking for? And if I know I'm looking for something, then why don't I know what I'm searching for? Why am I upsetting everyone's lives so greatly by putting my hands up in the air and crying out to Tom "I want another life, I don't want all this. I know there is more out there and I want it. I'm so sorry, I need to feel it, whatever it is!"

What is a perfect life? Does it really even exist? After all, I thought I had in theory what so many people dream of and was one of the luckiest girls I knew. I would have been, if I had been with the right man. Having moved to Spain, unbeknownst to myself I started a journey that I had no idea would lead me to here. I'm in a different place in my life now. I don't know if Tom and I can ever be in the same place again. I wish we could be. I wish we always had been. If he and I were destiny, I wouldn't feel like I do. I wouldn't have opened up my mind and heart to someone else in my life, surely?

I'm the most loyal of them all, the Leo, the lioness of the jungle. Loyalty is paramount to me. I would never, ever, do what I've done, and what I'm doing. How could I? How could I fall in love with another man? I'm married to a man who would do anything for his girls. They are everything to him so how on earth could I be taking his world apart in front of him. Why is it all so painful? Why am I crying?

Maybe I've been married to a man that wasn't destined to be my future. I think I've known it deep down, for a very long time. Even on our wedding night eight years ago I felt so lonely. We barely spoke. We didn't cuddle, kiss or even have one dance together. Every time

I looked for him he was never looking for me. We were busy entertaining everybody but each other. We were the 'entertainment', the delightful, great couple who made everyone happy, everyone proud. The whole day was this 'amazing' grand affair.

It was the party of all parties. But I remember the night, the day and the day after. I thought at the time "Does everyone that gets married feel like this?"

We worked really well together. We met doing an interiors job on the King's Road and hit it off immediately. We got on well and were thrown together in the midst of parties and fun in London, but within nine months we were engaged and I had moved with him an hour out of town to an 18th-century converted prison called 'The Locks,' up the end of a lane in the middle of the countryside. I was pregnant and awaiting the arrival of Daisy at the age of 24.

Our relationship grew to a point, and we were happy in the early years but over time, on so many profound occasions he would hurt me so deeply. Those memories regularly would come back to haunt me. Haunt me with the truth that we weren't going to grow old together. He wasn't the one.

He left me alone once when I was so ill that I hadn't moved off our bed for four days. Even after I begged him, crying for him not to go off to that meeting, he still did. He knew I felt like I was literally dying. I ended up ringing my own ambulance and spent two weeks in hospital with pneumonia, septicemia and gastroenteritis when Daisy was a mere nine months old.

Or the time when he made me walk alone in to a huge wedding reception because he didn't like what I was wearing. I'd sat in that bathroom and cried for a good half hour before I had the guts to go out and face their 'happy' day. These types of scenarios were ten a penny.

I was tired of size 16 knickers (five sizes too big for me) tied up with a knot in a plastic bag for my present under the tree, having had $200 thrown at them on Christmas Eve with no thought or any care. Or the presents that I'd bought him months in advance, which he gave away without even trying on. I had to sit at a Sunday lunch once only to see his father wearing the beautiful shirt that I had given Tom the week before.

I'd lost count of the number of birthday cards from him that he had got our au pairs to go and buy. Was I supposed to be grateful I even got one? I never cared about the cost or the size of the gift; I just wanted the thought occasionally. Call me picky, but all these things gradually damaged my love for him. Who says romance is dead? In our case rigor mortis had set in.

The irony is that if Tom and I hadn't got married we probably could have been great friends for life, but instead we would be more like the couple who ended up killing each other in the last scene of the movie 'War of the Roses,' where they both died hanging from the chandeliers. (In our case it would be a palm tree though…)

SEPTEMBER 13TH, 2004

I can judge my mind at the moment by the speed at which I'm deleting Tom's hideous texts. Whereas before I would read them several times, sinking into feeling awful. Desperate. Now I read them and delete them. They are gone as fast as they arrived.

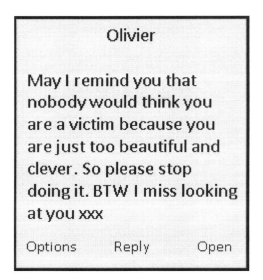

I wonder if there are other women who feel like me, who find themselves where they are 'supposed' to be in the eyes of society: married with children and the whole package, but then wondering, is that it? Now what happens? What if you just don't connect with your husband anymore, mentally or physically? Have you realized the dream, then asked yourself: Now what do I reach for? I didn't want to ever lose my sense of wonder, or magic, but I sure had with him.

It's been so long since I did something so big as to provoke my mind to thinking again. Not silence it anymore. Nothing is more powerful than a made-up mind. Being loved for who I am is what I've always searched for.

```
┌──────────────────────────────────┐
│                                  │
│              Olivier             │
│                                  │
│   If I don't see you soon I'm    │
│   going to kill somebody xxx     │
│                                  │
│                                  │
│                                  │
│                                  │
│                                  │
│                                  │
│   Options      Reply      Open   │
│                                  │
└──────────────────────────────────┘
```

I've started reading again for the first time in years, taking it all in and listening to myself, thinking even when I'm alone (which is a lot) that I'm not that lonely. Being here on the island forces me to face myself, by myself. My phone is the only contact I have with the outside world, and something that has such a bearing on my life. Text messages—never before have I written or received even a tenth of this type of texts. I've never been made to feel this good about myself by anyone. I feel beautiful, I feel funny, I feel challenging! I feel DESIRABLE! YIPPEE!

My brother Max in Japan, laughed on the phone last night when I told him about the last time I saw Olivier. I had picked him up in Barclay Square whilst I couldn't speak, I drove him around in circles laughing, my heart racing, as I didn't even know where I was going or was I parking? Oh, the rush of LOVE! I miss Max so much. God, I wish I had my big brother's arms to run into less than eight thousand miles away. He told me that I was like a diamond. That I shone and that even though life threw so much shit at me, I just kept on shining. I had to have it all! "Have what?" I asked. "Life," he said.

He told me that he and my other brother Jack were really proud of me. They were both concerned for me but that they would always support me, whichever path I decided to walk. It was one of the best, well timed, and honest conversations that we had ever had, one that I will always remember.

SEPTEMBER 15TH, 2004

I'm sitting in my friend Andre's villa overlooking the sea having some peace. Tom is here on the island and rather than allow him into my headspace or share any with him, I've left. He said he was coming to see the girls, even though he was here only four days ago and his only mission was chasing after me in his car, ringing me on the phone a hundred times an hour.

The more I separate myself, the more he feels lost. The more I'm honest about my feelings, the more it hurts him.

I told him from day one, when we separated back in June, that if I was ever going to be able to come back to him, I needed him to back off. It could take me weeks or even months, or I may never go back, but with him in my face how could I look at us, or our future objectively?

Everything I respectfully have asked him to do for me, for us, he hasn't. I pleaded with him. I just want him to leave me alone, give me room to breathe. His tactics aren't working but he is too blind and ignorant to listen to anyone.

I spent last weekend in Barcelona with Olivier. Our first, full weekend together was absolute heaven. From the second we arrived at the airport and jumped into the waiting car, it was like a fairy tale. He told me that he was very good at doing nothing. Excellent. For someone who is so clever, intelligent and so high-powered with his work, I was very impressed.

Lying by the pool with him in a totally quiet, tranquil, space together, he was indeed so relaxed, a total pleasure to be with. No phones. No stress. No pressure. We wondered around the beautiful city in the sunshine, holding hands and just being together. Going for dinner, sitting on huge soft cushions on the beach watching the sunset and drinking a lovely bottle of rosé, was by far the most fun I'd had for years.

How could I be so lucky? What price am I going to have to pay for this? Whilst I'm made to feel like the biggest bitch from hell, this surely proves I'm not that evil. If I was that awful, how could somebody so lovely want to be with ME?

When I got back from Barcelona, I walked in to see torn-up wedding photos around the bed with notes saying 'feeling guilty'? I replaced them with pictures of my best friends instantly.

> **Olivier**
> I wish I could be there to support you darling. It kills me watching you having to struggle so hard. i know that doesn't make it any easier for you right now. Just remember that I LOVE YOU!! xxx
>
> Options   Reply   Open

I can cope with all of it if I have his support helping me through this nightmare.

SEPTEMBER 16TH, 2004

In 29 days I leave for Peru to go and find myself. About bloody time! I'm going to camp in a jungle with a bunch of strangers, have late nights with shamans, take their poison to think straight, strip me of all my comforts to come back, hopefully with the strength to buck up and get on with the rest of my life.

The trip is led by a very special woman I've met called Viv who is a healer, a pioneer, who works on many levels to help souls that are struggling on their path. That's me all over! The minute I connected with her she read me like a book. No one has ever done that before, and I know she is going to have a very powerful effect on how I get through all this. She's a tough woman who takes no shit from anyone and I loved her from day one.

Her passion is to empower and guide those who are led to meet her for whatever reason, in mind, body, spirit and soul. She has the patience of a saint, the humor of a comedian alongside the most understanding temperament of a mother who looks out for you. She is going to help me heal the pain. Good. Might take her a while, she's got her work cut out with me!

I'm really excited. I'm so looking forward to being out of contact with Tom, but terrified about being separated from Olivier.

I wake up every single morning to lovely messages from him that help me get out of my bed to face the day ahead of me. So I wonder how I will survive without the consistent joy and appreciation he gives me.

I don't have a clue where I will be in three months'/six months' time. Where will I spend Christmas? Will I still be with my babies or will I have to sacrifice that pleasure since I'm the only wrong doer round these parts?

SEPTEMBER 17TH, 2004

Tom has no respect for me and rarely shows me any, so whilst he was spitting vile abuse at me again, I told him he had to stop calling me his 'darling heart,' especially in the same sentence.

"Why?" he said.

"Because I'm not your 'darling heart.'"

"Well whose are you then?"

"Somebody else's."

It was the cruelest thing I've ever said to anyone in my life. I don't want to be this person, but somehow now, I think after all these months of hell, it's the only way I'm going to get through to him that we are over. IT'S OVER!

It's been nearly four months now and he's still saying I'm his selfish, immoral wife who is not capable of thinking straight. He keeps telling me I am ruining the girl's lives, whereas I think I would if I stayed. There is no easy escape route. I've checked all the doors. Tom has the keys to most of them in his pocket. But I've got the key inside me, and it's the key to my own happiness. Ultimately to me being a happy person again.

We will all get through this and come out the other side. I will help the girls understand in years to come that it was the right decision.

I had to do it.

SEPTEMBER 18TH 2004

The girls and I picked Tom up at the airport last night, and when we got out of the car I saw a lovely old couple looking at Daisy and Amber running into the arms of their daddy. They both smiled so sweetly at us all. We looked like the 'perfect happy little family'. Little did they know we were everything but. We were in the midst of a hideous separation, couldn't even speak to each other, and the mother that they saw was in love with someone else, verging on suicidal and about to go directly to Departures once she had done the handover of the children.

I hope I will learn to have the knowledge to overcome my fears. I want to so badly.

Remember to breathe.

Remember to eat.

Keep going.

Carry on.

Focus on the good.

```
┌─────────────────────────┐
│         Olivier         │
│                         │
│  Last message – I can't wait │
│  to see you. I miss you. You │
│  are everything I want and I │
│  will dream about you every  │
│  night until I see you again │
│  xxx                    │
│                         │
│                         │
│  Options    Reply    Open │
└─────────────────────────┘
```

SEPTEMBER 25TH, 2004

It feels like forever since I have written in this book. After everything that's been going on none of it has killed me. In fact I feel stronger by the day. I have falling down days, but I think they aren't as common as they were.

Tom and I tried to go and talk about everything last night, and when we walked into a bar together I had this incredible feeling of genuinely not belonging to him. I didn't want to be there. And I didn't want to be with him.

I came back home and looked in the mirror to see a face that was drained and very sad. I took a long hot bath, sorted myself out and woke up in the morning feeling a lot better, thank god. I don't know how I'm doing this. Don't know much, but I do know that in three weeks I will be in deepest darkest Peru and will have time to think about EVERYTHING!

SEPTEMBER 28TH, 2004

Today I am having a bloody nightmare!! I don't seem to have even one stable consistent thought, plan, emotion or idea. I can't even begin to write down all that has happened in the last few days. It's just too much, and too bloody awful. I'm worn down and finding it very hard to focus. At least half a dozen friends were dragged once again into the firing line today alone by Tom desperately grasping any influence that would have on me to hurt me. He kept telling me my friends actually hate me for what I'm doing to him.

He's questioning me non-stop on my movements like a bloody policeman. Who? When? Why? What? I can't believe what I'm dealing with. I should have guessed it would be this hard. That he would make my life a living hell now.

It's been four and a half months and I'm plagued every single day. Every time my phone rings I flinch. How long is it going to be like this for? When will he turn a corner himself and LET ME GO! He keeps telling me to turn another corner. Turn one yourself! I want MY life back!!!

I wish that I was leaving tomorrow. I wish I could take the girls and go. Just be out of range.

I had an hour-long chat with my father the other night. The longer this goes on, the more he understands, accepts it and more importantly supports exactly what I'm doing and for all the right reasons.

```
        Olivier                    Olivier

I had a dream we were in    I know you will leave me
love. Tell me its true      one day so I need to just
darling? xxx                enjoy the time I have with
                            you until you bin me
                            forever xxx



Options   Reply   Open      Options   Reply   Open
```

OCTOBER 20TH, 2004

I saw Olivier last night. I flew to London for 10 hours. I changed from my 'on site' jeans and t-shirt, into a dress and heels, in the back of a black cab from Heathrow to Park Lane to meet him. Only the tiger knew as I'd put the girls to bed and was home by breakfast time. As I stood at the end of this long bar I watched him walk in and every time I set my eyes on him I just melt. I couldn't take my eyes off him. He showed me a photo of his beautiful girls. Could I move to Geneva?! Who knows where we will be in 6 months' time. My destiny is so open it's scary.

OCTOBER 22ND, 2004

I don't know whether I'm coming or going. I can't even cut up potatoes. Just can't think straight. What the hell was I thinking? I was possibly past the worst? The guilt, the uncertainty, the total blank future I have ahead. I feel completely ruined. Every little last piece of energy and strength has left me. Like a huge jigsaw puzzle I have thrown myself into the air and now I'm in pieces everywhere, without an edge to even start the picture.

I feel like I've been run over, buried and then dug up.

I had an awful run-in with Tom's parents, who turned up unannounced and uninvited in the kitchen here this morning. I walked down from upstairs to see Tom's father nosing through my paperwork on my desk. Then I saw the side of them both I never knew existed. It was really shocking.

"You must be delighted with your life now? Nice new Swiss boyfriend? Divorcing my son!? Do you seriously really think you can go it alone? Do you? You aren't capable of doing anything by yourself." They were both shaking with rage.

"When are you ever going to grow up and just stop thinking about yourself for once?" he barked at me.

''For the record, I'm the one that's actually trying to be the grownup right now," I snapped back. "Now if you don't mind, I'm busy."

I knew I didn't want to get into any further discussions with them or I would end up telling them all kinds of things they didn't need to know. They were devastated enough without making it even worse for them.

I guess my decade of being a loved and loving daughter-in-law just went out the window for good. My father-in-law, the 'ultimate Father Christmas' that I used to call him, now hated me. He couldn't have been bitter then if he'd tried. I had to say goodbye to all the years of good times we had shared, as it was never going to be like that again between us now. They loathed me for shattering the dream. I was always going to be the one that was guilty if our marriage ever failed, as Tom was born with golden bollocks in their eyes. Keep your rose-tinted spectacles on, safer that way.

The simple fact I have Daisy and Amber to focus on means I can't fall down. I can't give up. I can't surrender when it's wrong.

The girls are milking the cows as I write this. Tom is with them, trying to get me to go and see how lovely it is. The only reason I can't is because it's another emotional blackmail trip. I know how beautiful they are. I know how perfect that whole image is. That is what the ideal is all about. Lovely, innocent, perfectly happy beautiful girls, playing in the countryside, safe, happy and secure. How can I not go back just to keep that, for them? But what about 'us,' Tom?

I have legal papers right in front of me now. I can't believe this is my reality. I'm still fighting with the reality. I don't understand why I'm so sure. Where will I be? Where will the girls and I go? The dogs, my car, all our furniture? Will I have any money or will he try

and screw the girls and me over?

Am I mad? If I was going to snap out of it then why haven't I?

I am in love with a married man who is spending the weekend with his wife, his girls and

his friends, but it doesn't stop every part of me wanting to be with him right now.

I'm a mother that should only do the best for her children. Am I so selfish? What gives

me the right to change their lives so dramatically? Will they ever forgive me? Why can't I

just make it all better for everyone? Because I'm not included in what is best for everyone?

Or am I? Am I shooting myself in the foot, arm, heart or head? Is the grass greener? Isn't

ignorance bliss? If I hadn't met Olivier, would it be someone else that made me wake

up and dream again? When's a good time to turn your life upside down and inside out?

Doesn't it get even deeper rooted and even harder to do?

I'm so tired. I'm not thinking straight.

```
┌─────────────────────────────────┐
│              Olivier          ˅ │
│                                 │
│  I hate being apart from you    │
│  FYI xxx                        │
│                                 │
│                                 │
│                                 │
│                                 │
│                                 │
│                                 │
│   Options      Reply      Open  │
└─────────────────────────────────┘
```

OCTOBER 24TH, 2004

Tom has just gone. I had locked up and gone to bed only to be woken up by him at 1 a.m. trying to get in, a drunk and possessed madman, who was asking me all about Olivier AGAIN.

"Is our marriage really over? Why can't you turn a corner? Look at you. You are so frail and weak looking. You look terrible. You aren't thinking straight about yourself." He went on and on. I went back to bed and he left all the doors open and drove off with a screech of tires on the driveway. I didn't get back to sleep until nearly 4 a.m., then I woke up with him standing by my bed again, straight in to me. "You are ruining my life," etc., etc. I had to take him to the airport and listen to the same shit, the same words, all over again. But in the back of my mind I knew that today would be the last time I see him before I left for Peru.

I was worrying last night that I felt so drained, I wasn't sure how I was going to make it through the day. Let alone another week before I leave. This time next week I will be in the air, miles above the world, on my way to brief freedom. I've got such a strong suspicion that whatever happens when I'm out there, is going to change my life forever.

Tom asked me today what 'spirituality' is. He thinks I'm so screwed up that I will come back from Peru with a brain. Lets hope so.

I'm thinking about my beautiful Olivier. When he says to me "You are so much better than me," I think he's so crazy. What does he say that for? If anything he is so much better than me! He is so different from any man I've met before. He has so many qualities that are special. He is so calm, so witty, so intelligent, so well read, so interesting, so affectionate, so romantic and so attractive.

He looked up lots of information for me on Peru tonight. I love that. He is so interested in what I'm going to be doing, what I'm going to be seeing. Interested in me and where I'm going in my life. What makes him think so much of me? Is it just the fact that I'm so unusual to him? Or is it because I drown him in love, affection and attention? Whatever it is that he finds so attractive, I have no idea.

Olivier

You think I would spend the precious time I have with my children thinking about you if I didn't care about you? You are my obsession! xxx

Options   Reply   Open

Olivier

Big mistake if you think I'm not in love with you. I'm crazy about you
xxx

Options   Reply   Open

OCTOBER 28TH, 2004

I'm in Paris. I had to come to see him as he is here on business. I had to see him again before I go to Peru, otherwise it would be three weeks or more. And I know I can't do that long! I was just thinking, thank god this is a thick book, because I have a lot to write about....

So here I am. In the same hotel we stayed in back in July. Utterly romantic and I have just opened a present he had sent here for my arrival. A delicate silver necklace, with three blue topaz droplets. I love it. Olivier is flying in from London and will be here soon. Then tomorrow I go to London for an appointment at hospital to check out a pain in my tummy I've had for weeks and then on to Peru on Sunday.

Saying goodbye to my babies this morning in Menorca was heart wrenching, as I've never been away from them for two weeks, but they are excited to have daddy to themselves with late nights, chocolate biscuits, no rules and nonstop fun.

I set the alarm extra early so we could all cuddle in bed without having to rush before I took them to school. We did each other's hair as always and had long chats about what I had lined up for them whilst I was away on my adventure. It couldn't have been lovelier.

Daisy's lent me her Hello Kitty rucksack so that I can use it and think of her. I'm so proud of them. I feel like such a crap mother but I think that I'm helping them to become confident, strong and independent little girls, if nothing else. They are very contented. They have so few tears.

I can't believe I've got here. To this point of sorting the girls, house, animals, everything, having very little help and no support over the past few months, along with my consistent daily punishments, it has all nearly finished me off.

> **Olivier**
> I know I'm not funny and too quiet at times but I can only improve as the woman I love is very stimulating and so lovely! I find it incredible you love me so much but I do believe it now xxx
>
> Options   Reply   Open

> **Olivier**
> I'm so happy you like your present. I'm going to miss you so much my darling. Travel safely and I hope you find what you are looking for out there. I love you ! xxx
>
> Options   Reply   Open

We enjoyed a wonderful dinner on the Champs Elysee with thousands of sparkling lights on both sides of the avenue. It really was fairy-tale romancing. He told me how great I looked as we walked back to our hotel, but my heels were hurting like hell, so much to his amusement I walked barefoot the whole way back.

OCTOBER 31ST, 2004

Heathrow—Destination Spiritual Adventure in Peru.

I'm four hours into my flight to Lima, surrounded by the fourteen new travel companions

I met with Viv, for the first time at the gate at 4 a.m. My least favorite time of the day, especially with strangers! I feel tired, scared and seem to be going further and further out of my comfort zone. I went to the back of the plane and cried for what seemed like hours asking myself what the hell am I doing? What have I let myself in for?

No drinking. No smoking. No girlfriends. No lover. No phone. Hmmm.

FIFTEEN LONG AND MILDLY UNCOMFORTABLE HOURS LATER

We arrived in Lima at last surrounded by poverty and casinos. Our hotel's lovely so we just need to get our heads down for the night before our adventure really starts to kick in.

My roommate Sally is a fabulous lady, whom I knew I would bond with the second I met her. Long blonde hair down her back, huge eyes and the biggest smile with the most infectious laugh I've heard in years. A lovely genuine girl, I discovered when we lay in our beds in the dark chatting for hours about our lives. It's good to know we are going to get along and have a giggle. Most importantly she makes me feel sane with the laughs between us over emotions, love and men.

6 am. Mmmmmm, yuck. Shower and breakfast. I have a feeling this is going to be an extraordinary experience. I've tuned in to some really good people and I've been laughing a lot for a change! (Good humor is something I've been missing, my god it's good to feel like that again) Everyone is here for his or her own reasons; Their own journeys—who knows where this is going to lead us all?

Amongst the group there is a neatly dressed, incredibly stylish looking, wealthy lawyer, four children; all at private schools, huge estate, handsome well-respected husband; she wanted out.

There was also a powerful man who owns a large recruitment company who reminded me of the lion from 'The Wizard of Oz': king of the jungle, yet as meek as a mouse. Henpecked to within an inch of his life by a wife who drained his bank account to sustain her desire and need for Tiffany diamonds. The type of woman I could never relate to who did nothing but play golf, shop and lunch with girlfriends, whilst spending her husband's hard-earned money. No conscience whatsoever. I would hazard a guess that there isn't an awful lot of sex going on either.

A well rounded, ruddy faced woman with no family or relatives, with hair like a poodle, who laughs at everything. A couple that seems one of the most ill-matched pair that I've ever met. She is hardnosed and wants to talk nonstop about irrelevant, uninteresting, rubbish while he seems far brighter and gentle, with a completely opposite vibe.

And Sally, who is just confused. Probably just suffering with a midlife crisis, she truly loves her husband. I wanted to be in her shoes.

Last night was my first night in the jungle. In fact my first night in a jungle ever! The very first time I'm out of range from everyone in every way. During the boat journey down the Amazon everything started to take a new dimension. I looked around observing all the different people I'm here with. No one was talking. Maybe we were all scared. There was an eerie anticipation amongst us. Everyone was trying to take it all in, the unknown was ahead of us all.

I never imagined the Amazon to be so beautiful, lush, alive and bursting with nature.

We arrived at our lodge right on the river to our 'open to the elements' huts. We had a relaxed evening and were all in bed by 9:30 only for me to be awoken at midnight with the most awful nightmares. I was being chased in cars and on foot, trapped with my passport torn into pieces.

I got tangled up in my mossy net and became conscious with Sally reassuring me with her hands on my shoulders. I cried and cried. I couldn't even breathe. Surreal. I really WAS thousands of miles away in the middle of a jungle with a bunch of complete strangers.

"What time is it?" I eventually asked.

"Whatever time you want it to be," she smiled gently back at me. All I could see was the whites of her eyes and teeth in the darkness.

She guided me outside and we sat there under the moon with more monkeys squawking and bugs flying by than you can imagine, wrapped up tightly in our sheets.

Out of adversity you have to find humor and the tears as always turned to laughter when I realized I was safe and untouchable. I can't actually remember the last time I felt safe. It's good to be around new people right now. This was going to be an amazing voyage.

The next morning I woke up really early again in my bare surroundings with just a wall between my bed and a dripping shower, home to some really large disturbing bugs.

I decided to get up as I'd slept enough to walk down to the river where I found 'Clint.' His real name was the same as my husband's, (which I couldn't cope with hearing at all) so I'd renamed him already by the cowboy hat permanently attached to his head.

He'd been up for hours having bad dreams in the night too. It dawned on me then he and all of us shared one main thing in common. It seemed we all knew what we wanted but all of us were held back by one single thing. Fear. Fear of letting go. Fear of the impact of our decisions on other people's lives. Doing what we were doing was taking ourselves as far away from our comforts as possible, striving for courage, stripping us bare to the naked truth.

I feel like I'm part of an alternative family here right now, very detached.

We are all helping and supporting each other. There are very interesting dynamics going on within the group.

The mysterious single woman in her early fifties seemed to have blanked me for no apparent reason from the time we met at the airport, so I decided to take my coffee and sit next to her. After an awkward one-sided conversation, she told me that I looked just like her daughter who had died a few months before, hence my presence there was painful to her, which was obviously the reason she was on this trip. We talked about her, the life that was so cruelly cut short and her grandchildren who were left behind. I hugged her for several minutes as she held back her tears. I will never forget it and from that moment on we were friends. I was the enemy no more.

I feel very lonely without my contact with Olivier. I think about him all the time, wondering if he's thinking about me. I lay in a hammock yesterday absorbing the jungle and I knew if we were together in that hammock that we would fit into each other's space perfectly. We would be locked into each other and we wouldn't even need to speak.

This afternoon I had my first meeting with Mateo, the shaman, in an empty roofless hut with two single rusty old beds. I had often tried to imagine what a shaman would look like and Mateo looked every bit the part. His face was carved in history and wisdom. Huge deep brown eyes looked right into me with a calmness that was almost overwhelming. We sat cross-legged opposite each other talking about all the worries I had and the FEAR! The bloody fear! We discussed it all right down to why I was here in the first place. It felt strange to be talking about myself, and my feelings as I'd been suppressing them even to myself for a long time. It was all very interesting although the constant spitting of his tobacco slightly distracted me. I've got a real aversion to seeing people spit! I'm here to teach myself I can do anything I want with my life if I just believe in myself and trust my feelings. That's all? Easy then.

November 2nd, 2004

Two days later and I'm already feeling like I'm starting to get a grip. Being around the people I'm with is a huge benefit to sorting my brain out a little more right now. I'm lying in my open-air hut listening to all the sounds of the jungle. I was awoken this morning by a laughing monkey in my doorway. I laughed back. What a way to start the day.

There is never silence here. The heavens opened earlier. The rain came down with such monumental force it was almost like it was clearing the way for us. Giant leaves acting like umbrellas as the water poured off them. It was so loud, so beautiful, and so intense. I sat by the Amazon for hours watching it flowing past carrying with it trees and branches. I stared with fascination as a large island covered in grass floated by! I could sit by the river for hours with its powerful, silent current, so calming.

I watched the reflections of the trees on the rippling puddles where the last drops of rain were falling. Giant red butterflies fluttered noisily around me as I witnessed all manner of ants rushing up and down the struts of my hut. Nature, up to my neck in it! Frogs that sound the size of cows croaking away, huge lizards were waddling around, millions of birds chatting away all at once. I sat on a jetty with my feet in the water until I was warned that I could lose them at any moment.

Apparently piranhas make fast work of feet with a fine pedicure.

I've just realized why I haven't been to sleep today. The fear of having more nightmares I think. Stupid I know, but what I experienced last night was so real I don't want to go back there. I think that's what it is yet all the others have slept in preparation as we were asked to do.

I'm about to take part in the Ayahuasca ceremony tonight. I'm taking the root from the plants of the jungle that the Incas took to clear their minds. Ayahuasa is a quantum leap for spiritual development. It's not a drug; it is a tool for transformation. It opens the left hand side of your brain; your senses and heart, to dimensions that you didn't know were possible. As it does this, it destroys your ego. You will undoubtedly find that when you try to go back, you can't. You will see the world differently, more clearly. It gives you a glimpse into the deep subconscious; a part we don't know exists. Frightening. The side effects would include vomiting major style, and diarrhea like never before to help release the toxins in our bodies.

(To release my lifetime's worth of toxins I will need a gallon's worth!) Oh dear...

We are all doing it also and supposed to do it tomorrow night too. Without a doubt this is the only place to do something as powerful as this in life (not in Cadogan Gardens, London SW3, as it has now become fashionable). I'm very excited but also nervous with anticipation. I wonder how I will feel tonight. What will clearing my mind be like? What will I be left with?

DAY 4 IN THE JUNGLE. POST THE FIRST CEREMONY.

We all met at 7 p.m. prior to the ceremony at 9:30. We all sat around drinking tea (I loathe tea) after the third meal of the day. Can't remember having three meals a day – ever. I'm actually putting on weight in the jungle! We all laughed so much once again to the point I had tears pouring down my cheeks as we discussed hidden cameras with it all being a set up for some bizarre reality show that we would be watching on the plane home.

I think the realization of everything is hitting home prior to this ceremony with everyone. We are all a long way from home and I'm actually pretty scared. It's almost impossible to describe this environment and the scene I'm in the middle of. Whatever is going to happen to me tonight feels so powerful that I can only rest without closing my eyes, listening to my iPod.

We were all dressed in our whites when we met at the ceremonial space—a huge open hut a little walk into the jungle with a central post. Our twelve mattresses had been laid out on the floor like a clock around it, with several feet between each one of us. After a few minutes of meditation, we were told to close our eyes. Edith, one of our guides, came around us one by one putting drops of this potion on our arms, foreheads, backs of our neck and hands to protect us. Protect us from what, I wondered?

We all lay there in complete silence and darkness. There were only two oil lamps outside in the open of the jungle. We then had the first dose of the drink, which tasted absolutely revolting, hideous. Somewhere between the worst cough mixture you've ever had and something I can't describe. I almost threw up as it hit the back of my throat. One by one we downed it in one fell swoop. I didn't want to close my eyes, as I was afraid of falling asleep so I kept them wide open. Being a control freak with my own brain and not letting go, I knew in the back of my mind it might take a while to allow myself to feel it, so I waited and waited.

After what was probably half an hour, one of the women across the room started to fly, cry out and wail, thrashing her arms and legs around. We had all been told earlier many times to detach ourselves from what may be going on around us tonight, to concentrate on our own experience but as she started screaming at the top of her voice it was impossible for me to let go. Gradually more and more of the group started making sounds to the point I felt I was observing a scene from 'One Flew Out of the Cuckoo's Nest'!

Clint was lying next to me. I could see tears starting to roll down his lion's cheeks and his chest was rising with deep breaths trying to resist his emotion. All I wanted to do was get up and go and hug him. I hated seeing him suffering yet I wasn't allowed to do anything but just watch. Sally was on the far side of the room and I was worrying about her too. She was next to the poodle who had been barking all evening and was now screaming at the top of her voice again.

Viv came over and whispered to me, "Half your problem in life is that you spend so much of your time obsessing and worrying about other people's problems. Detach yourself now. Think of only you. Everyone is fine. Just concentrate on yourself."

I lay there looking up at the roof of the hut watching the weak shadows moving around with thousands of fireflies flashing. In the distance I began to hear rain and before I knew it started to pour down just as the potion started to rush through my veins, like a thunder bolt from the ends of my fingers, to running down my spine through to the tips of my toes. I felt this need not to have anything against my skin so I took off the necklace that Olivier had given me in Paris and held it tightly in my hand.

It was like a director of the jungle had clapped his hands, ordering thunder and lightning with the most dramatic effects for us all to spin out to. I started laughing for no reason.

I was still so preoccupied by all the crying, moaning and head-shaking going on all around me, along with seeing some of us being guided in and out to be sick. Two different people were seeing the same visions of spirits coming into our space and were terrified of them.

I sat up to watch them all, absolutely transfixed.

Viv told me to lie down, to close my eyes and be quiet. She had a stern look in her eyes and I knew she meant it. Mateo was chanting, the rain was now pelting down with the heavens lit up with the lightening and as I closed my eyes for the first time I felt tears starting to roll gently down my cheeks. Here we go! Oh my god…

I stroked the necklace and clung to a vision of Olivier. I remember thinking that the necklace resembled our love for each other. Beautiful, fragile and so delicate that if I squeezed it too tightly it would break, but right at that moment it was giving me a security I needed badly. I really started to cry then.

The shamans were pacing in the darkness slowly around the foot of our beds smoking the peace tobacco. I had to wave over through my tears to Viv. I needed her. I needed someone as I was losing control of my body and mind. I was desperate for reassurance. She came over, put her hand in mine and lovingly touched my head in a way a mother strokes her child. I could feel sweat starting to cover me as my stomach churned like a cement mixer, then I started being sick in the bucket by my mattress.

"Sick him up, darling," she said. I couldn't stop myself again, and again, until I collapsed back on the mattress. She shook out and carefully placed her sarong gently over me, which in my imagination felt like a silk duvet of security.

"Here are the tears after the laughter," she smiled. I could barely speak or even focus on her through the tears but I remember asking her if I'd ever be free? Would I really be able to free myself of the life I had, enough to do what I needed to do? What I was going to try to do was against all odds. I was going to have to seriously fight for this dream.

At that exact moment like an impossible puzzle everything seemed to fall into place.

I can't write in words the intense leap of understanding I had, but a power flowed right through me then, with a clear acceptance of what was going on with me, with my life. Numbingly clear thought. A profound moment.

For what was probably another hour, I just lay there taking it all in and breathing gently.

I had at last blocked out all the distraction around me. I was in my own strange world entirely. Tom had lost me forever, I was never coming back. It was too late but I knew then for the first time it was OK to be truthful to myself. I would find the courage I desperately needed to deal with changing my life. I'd get through this somehow and so would he. I'm here facing the truth of my unhappiness. I have to get closer to being at peace with myself. I've spent months, days and nights being tortured, chased, tormented, punished and blamed for doing the wrong thing, for making big mistakes. Could I really be that wrong?

I was straight, sober and felt the clearest I've ever been in my life. I wanted to leave this space with everyone else now to be alone. I was the first to leave the ceremony with the craziness behind. I walked back to my hut by myself down the flamed pathway to lie and listen to the jungle once more. I eventually fell into what felt like a deep meditation but I was definitely still conscious.

After only three hours I got up and went to sit and watch the river. Most of the group were still on their mattresses in the ceremonial space, still spinning out even after the whole night's experiences. I really hoped Clint and Sally were OK. I was very tired now. In reality I've probably only had six or seven hours over the last few nights yet I feel awake inside, very awake.

I miss Olivier so much it actually hurts me. I wondered again as I always did, was he thinking about me? If when I returned he had changed his mind, would I be able to deal with it? I might just be able to deal with everything now. I wasn't leaving my husband for him, I never was, but it seemed to the outside world the only explanation for my actions.

I felt empowered for the first time in years.

DAY FIVE IN THE JUNGLE

Last night I did the whole thing again as planned. Most of us did as the theory being, when you take it the second time; you go in your head directly to where you want to be, where you need to be. I had already seen enough, though. There wasn't much room for more revelations. The penny had already dropped, I'd felt it land but I wasn't going to back out now.

Sally and I laughed like little girls before we went in to lie on our beds on the floor and swallow the Ayahuasca. It was far more relaxed, the whole evening was different.,

No storms, no screaming, no moaning and no laughing either. It was very quiet. Several of the group (thankfully including the poodle) couldn't handle the second time around and had been high until lunchtime, so had bowed out earlier in the day. When Mateo sat by my bed healing me I felt nothing at all yet the girl lying next to me saw this great pain being lifted off me. Maybe that was it, the crushingly powerful decisions had been made and somehow I felt a release.

I quietly went to leave and Viv lay down on my bed. She told me the next morning that there was an amazing glow of colors floating around the space I'd been in on the mattress for the rest of the night. Nice. Nice to know I left a good feeling behind, I obviously had enough to share around! Maybe I was finally letting go.

DAY SIX IN THE JUNGLE

I slept really deeply for the first time since being away, in fact the best I had done in months. Alberto, one of the shamans, took us on a jungle walk where we learnt all about the trees and plants which was pretty interesting, but the real fun for me was taking the longest vine I could see and swinging on it backwards and forwards across the wide river. Tarzan's Jane! Nobody else had the courage, as what lay beneath in the water varied from hungry crocodiles to leeches, but I loved the rush so I did it again, and again, like I did when I was a child. Something inside me wasn't scared anymore.

I played football with some sweet local kids in a clearing, returned for lunch, packed up and said goodbye to our lodge, our hosts and headed back up the Amazon to the city of Iquitos, and back to a little more civilization. Maybe my phone will work?

On arrival in Iquitos I had a signal but no messages. NO MESSAGES? I felt totally flat.

I called the girls but they were already in bed when the babysitter answered. I text Tom saying I would call them tomorrow. He instantly responded and then started calling me nonstop. I got a rush of heat all over, like a kind of panic so I turned my phone off. Babysitters and psycho husbands weren't on my menu tonight.

A FEW HOURS LATER

I'm now on the plane back to Lima to be back in time for dinner as we are up and out at 6 a.m. for our next adventure. I'm hoping I will hear from Olivier tomorrow. I don't know which country he's in, or what he's doing or more importantly how he's feeling. I wish I did. I awoke to him calling me as I snuggled in my duvet, wrapping myself in his beautiful, peaceful voice. He'd sent lots of messages, which I hadn't got. It made me feel better when he told me he was missing me desperately. That makes two of us. I told him about the ceremonies which he was fascinated by. One of the things I love most about him is he's so smart because he's ALWAYS learning. I love that. We talked about my journal that I'm writing. He said he wants to read it. Mmmm not sure what he will make of it by the time I've finished it, if I ever do?

I spoke to my babies tonight. It was so great to hear their little voices. Daisy reminded me (at the age of 6!!) "Mummy, never be afraid to be who you are." How can a six year old come out with something so profound? She's such a smart little girl. I love them both so much. It's good to know they are safe and happy right now and having a great time with daddy. I'm looking forward to seeing them again when I'm stronger, more able to be mentally committed to them after the relentless, exhausting months of hell I've been through. I feel like I've been such a crap mother recently. I hate myself for that.

```
┌──────────────────────────────┐
│                              │
│           Olivier            │
│                              │
│  I'm so attracted to you I   │
│  want to make love to you    │
│  for a week non-stop soon    │
│  xxx                         │
│                              │
│                              │
│                              │
│  Options    Reply     Open   │
└──────────────────────────────┘
```

Viv called the doctor here in Lima earlier to look at my stomach pains that are getting worse. Nobody knows what is wrong with me, as I've been having pains for the last six months. I'm sure it all related to stress and worry. The doctor didn't tell me but he told her that my body was incredibly anxious; strange, because I felt pretty good by then. These people and their intuition are quite unbelievable to me. I was extremely dehydrated so I had an injection for the cramp. Apparently I'm blocking it all out as my survival technique. Women hold all their emotions in their tummies. I was doubled up in pain later on another flight and now I'm feeling very weak, like I could sleep for a week.

I need a massage badly.

DAYS LATER

I'm back in Cuzco, having been to the very top of the majestic temple Machu Picchu. It truly is one of the Seven Wonders of the World. The energy, the power with the immensity of the mountains virtually took my breath away. There's very little oxygen up there too! I'd never seen anything in nature as powerful before. It was incredibly peaceful, being right up there in the clouds. A strange silence surrounds you.

A silence so intense it makes every thought seem louder.

Yesterday it was very misty and raining. One minute the mountains were there, the next they had vanished in the sky again. Viv told me it was sometimes best to wait for the mist to go before making choices or decisions as the mist always goes eventually, and then you can see clearly. This was true and today there was stunning sunshine without a cloud in sight. I sat on a huge rock for hours staring at the magnificence of the mountains, feeling like a bird. I was so high just listening to my music. The ceremony was held in 'the crystal cave', a space that holds the energy of nurturing and total peace. When we are at peace we can enjoy our surroundings and find the courage to move on.

The purpose of this was to reconnect us with mother earth and birth mother, it helps us look back, readjust our souls and imagine our future.

> ## Olivier
>
> Every hour of every day I am asking myself if I am capable of leaving everything for you xxx
>
> Options   Reply   Open

It really surprised me to read that in black and white. He had a lot to think about, and then again, so did I. The decisions I was making were based on my children and me; I wasn't putting everyone in a critical position purely based around my love for him.

I couldn't and I wouldn't. These huge answers and solutions I was looking for had to be based around faith and not fear.

We had the Alignment ceremony up at the ancient ruins of Pisac. This was the most powerful of all the ceremonies for me (without being off my head on Ayahuasca!).

All the flowers we laid on the mountain represented an offering to Mother Nature. It was a very beautiful scene. The mountain children that had followed us all up to the top just sat and watched with fascination. They had such peace in their big brown eyes. I loved seeing them excitedly trying on all the clothes and shoes I had brought them as a small present, things that the girls had grown out of. They were very sweet, so pleased and happy.

Towards the end, as people started to slowly leave the mountain, the shaman asked me to wait behind and to lie on my back against the earth. He could feel the deep pain in my tummy. I lay there, he didn't touch me but I felt this energy through the palms of his old hands. I was grounded to the spot. I felt no pain at all for hours after, only numbness. Weird.

SEVERAL DAYS LATER

I haven't written in this journal for days. I haven't found the energy or the space to be alone and write. I'm so run down because I never allow myself to let go at home in my normal life. I never switch off and all these things have come out of my body all at once here, but I think I may have turned a corner.

After ten whole days of ignoring my husband's calls for my own sanity, I spoke to him. A tiny part of me was hoping, imagining us having a half-decent conversation with him being semi nice to me. Maybe he was sorry too. Maybe he would share just a little blame. But he was everything I dreaded him being, everything he always was. Everything I wished he wasn't. He talked over me, interrupted me and barely listened to a word I said in the whole twenty minutes.

Most of it was a blur as my brain was full of positivity after all the healing, so I wasn't processing it. I didn't want to hear all the repeated, loaded, guilt-ridden crap coming out of his mouth. There were still no offers of any responsibility whatsoever for the collapse of our marriage. It was my fault entirely and I had lost my mind—situation normal.

If only he was capable of opening his mind for once. Be willing to learn some humility and allow me to express myself without constant interruption. He never listened to me, so he never learnt how I thought, how I really felt. That made it impossible to grow together. It was becoming more and more apparent that we were growing even further apart in every way. How could I ever imagine being able to rebuild when he was so goddamn perfect and the entire mess we were in was all down to me? It takes two to tango, baby. I wanted to scream down the phone at him that I'd given him everything I possibly could and it was still never enough, but I didn't have the energy or the will. The woman he wanted me to be was a woman I could never be. That was just the way it was.

I'm really pleased we spoke then, even though I felt depressed afterwards.

The disappointment of never hearing what I needed to hear from him, never seemed to get easier. It feels good to be truthful though. It's feeling good to free myself. I have given him every opportunity to win me back. Prove he's worth it. Show me something to prove 'we' are worth working at. Thank god I feel stronger everyday with my decision. He doesn't want 'me' for me and I don't want him.

I can't wait to see my babies. I miss them so much. I feel like I've got a lot of making up to them to do. I've been so preoccupied in the confusion and shit I'm in. I can't wait to cuddle them again, sit and read stories, go for lovely walks with the dogs and generally regroup. I spoke to them again earlier. Daisy asked me to tell her one of my stories so I told her about me being 'Jane' in the jungle, swinging from the vines across the river.

She loved hearing about that. I can't wait to tell her and Amber about all the other things I've done here that they will enjoy hearing about.

> **Olivier**
>
> You are the most interesting and beautiful person I have ever met and that is why I am thinking about divorce every day. I miss you so much darling
> xxx
>
> Options   Reply   Open

It really upset me reading this, as I felt his pain. No one could relate to it more than me and I felt really guilty for where he was. But that is our lives right now and we were both rolling the dice flat out. We were each as guilty as the other for the situation we were in.

LAST DAYS IN PERU

Well, I'm now on a plane from Cuzco to Lake Titicaca. We were escorted to the airport in an open-backed, bomb squad police wagon with four armed guards. There is a strike here today so they have blocked all the roads. And so that's how we got here, thanks to Viv using her contacts! Very, very funny looking at the 'Brady Bunch' being thrown around in the back. Especially looking at the poodle, still obsessed with her hair being in place, who had been on the loo for the past week following her 'Madawaska' experience as she called it, trying to hold on for dear life. This just topped it all off for her!

We are off to the lake for the San Pedro ceremony tomorrow. San Pedro is a cactus that you take to open your conscience to a lighter side of yourself, making you more aware of the spirit of nature, giving you a feeling of uplifting. It enables you to focus and lifts depression. All I know is that we will be spending nearly all day on the water, eating sweeties, as apparently that's all you want to do whilst you cry and laugh the day away, which I'm really looking forward to!

November 17th, 2004

It's been almost a week since I wrote in this book ,and so much has happened I don't even know where to start. First of all, the final part of my trip in Peru was the boat trip on Lake Titicaca where I nearly died. We all took the San Pedro by the side of the lake.

Two of us swam in the freezing water, which was a mere 12 degrees! If you can swim even for thirty seconds, it is supposed to be the best boost possible for your immune system. The sun was very hot as most sat in their bathers, not daring to put even one toe in.

It was going really well before I foolishly took a call from Tom just as I got on the boat only to hear him ranting that he was going to chase me everywhere, that I would never escape from him. In the frame of mind I was in with the San Pedro in my system my panic stations started pumping, draining my strength and clarity to zero and the day went south from there onwards.

On the three-hour boat journey back to land and our hotel, I fell monumentally downhill.

I was so out of it, had such bad sunstroke and my bones were so frozen that I don't remember being carried off the boat over the shoulder of Clint.

I was laid on a bed, on watch, wrapped in a dozen alpaca blankets and spent the entire night on oxygen. This was hideous, but an important lesson in itself, probably the best lesson of all to show me how much the way Tom treats me gets into my system.

It affects me hugely, mentally and physically.

I then flew back the 27 grueling hours across the world to Olivier.

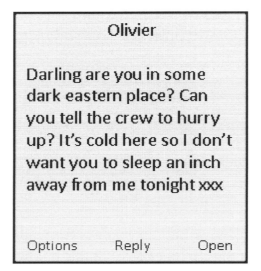

And then…

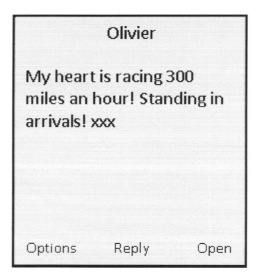

When I read that message I was in the ladies, splashing cold water on my face and

running a brush through my hair, looking in a mirror for the first time in days at baggage

reclaim. Jesus, look at the state of me! So this is what you look like when you've just been

on a wild adventure to find yourself then? Ha! He will look divine and I will walk through looking like a homeless bag lady. Excellent! (But I was so sick with excitement I could have been floating two feet off the floor.)

Jules

Are you back darling? Did you find yourself?? Can't wait to hear all about it!! xxxxxxx

Options   Reply   Open

I said goodbye to all my new-found friends and got a taxi into London. We talked, kissed and cuddled the entire journey and spent the evening sitting on the floor together in his apartment sharing my crazy experiences. Every time I see him I think it can't possibly get any stronger, and it just does.

I flew back to Menorca the next morning to be met by the girls standing alone with Tom having already gone through to Departures the other side of the airport. My babies! Hooray, we are back together. The longest we have ever been apart – fifteen days. We got back to the house to find that Danny, our live-in Kiwi who had been working on the house for the past year, had been moved out under duress whilst I was away.

I knew immediately it was another tactic to hurt me, there was no other reason to get him out other than to make me even more isolated and alone. Tom had been staying there with the girls, with him, whilst I was gone and the house was in a disgusting state when I walked in. Washing up was left piled high in the sink, a pile of rank-smelling dog poo on the floor in the kitchen left for me to clear up, and wet, rotting clothes in piles. There were the usual, complimentary pictures of him and I, on and even in my bed.

Great. Welcome home darling.

I sat and just cried on the floor in the kitchen when the girls were fast asleep that night.

I had somehow held it together for them all evening, hiding the pictures before they saw them and binning the letters. I was majorly jet-lagged, tired, shocked to be back in my new world, that I had created now, with the largest bump on record.

Olivier had rung within minutes of my arriving back to check I got home OK. I told him a lot of what had been going on between Tom and me over the past few months. Just to what extent I was being punished daily, but he doesn't need to know all the crap. It's all so alien to him as he is such a gentlemen. He was shocked enough, by the little I told him.

I thought about picking up the suitcase, packing one for the girls and heading straight out the door. Where to though? I wasn't leaving yet. I wouldn't be bullied out until we had arranged everything.

I cleaned the house from top to bottom, made it our beautiful home again, and got over my jet lag. So lovely to see the girls by myself and spend time getting normality back (what ever that is now). Danny came over to the house when Tom went back to the UK and I asked him if he wanted to come back to stay, so we didn't have to be alone down that drive in the deep winter months. I'd lost count of the amount of times the generator would blow up or run out of fuel and we were constantly plunged into darkness and cold. Tom refused to get a generator that was powerful enough for the size of Bona Ventura.

You can bet if he lived here we would have one but that would make our lives here comfortable. That wasn't his plan. The plan was for the house to double up as Amityville Horror for my benefit only, so that I would give up, surrender, and take him back.

Danny was always around to help fix the generator, fighting the wind and rain in the darkness. We were screwed without him around and Tom knew it. Not to mention the feeling of security as I hated being so remote. He agreed to come home, which made Amber ecstatic and Daisy and I, along with both the dogs, very relieved and happy. He had become part of the family and the girls loved him like a big brother. Plus he got fed lovely food every day, enjoyed the manor house and pool with his own top floor, and was generally mothered by me doing all his washing etc. We all got on well and had many fun times too. The decision was a no brainer. He didn't want to move out in the first place.

```
┌─────────────────────────────────┐
│            Olivier              │
│                                 │
│  You know I love you. We        │
│  need each other. It's very     │
│  simple xxx                     │
│                                 │
│                                 │
│                                 │
│                                 │
│                                 │
│   Options      Reply      Open  │
└─────────────────────────────────┘
```

I flew back to London as planned with the girls the following weekend, picked up a hire car at Gatwick to drive straight to my parents, which was always my plan. I'd been thinking a lot about them both on my journey. I had a very productive evening with them, once the girls were in bed, explaining a lot about my life, what was going on, my experiences in Peru and all that they were unaware of. I tried not to cry but couldn't help it when I told Dad that half the reason I think I had stayed for so long with Tom, was because I was afraid of disappointing him. He stood up, walked around the table and cried too whilst he bear-hugged me.

I'd only seen him cry once, which was when my mother left him when I was ten years old and even then, he never knew I saw him. He wasn't the type of man to cry, especially in front of a daughter. He was my rock. He had always showed me strength, even in times when it would have almost been impossible for him in the past. I admired my father more than anyone in the world. He had put himself through college having done every paper round, every milk round, and any job he could get with his father at war, along with studying late into the night. He'd gone on to win a scholarship into Cambridge, having hitchhiked to get there, and had worked his ass off his whole life in order to selflessly put all four of his children through public school and give us all wonderful childhoods. I was a very lucky girl to have such a great Dad. We stood and hugged for what felt like ages. Both him and my stepmother Katie (whom I shared everything with and whom I was very close to) said they could see the real me coming back, that it would all work out.

They could also see how much I'd learned in Peru about myself.

We talked about Olivier too as they asked many questions, naturally. I told them he was one of the loveliest men I'd ever met, that I was very much in love with him but that I had no idea whether or not we would end up together. I wasn't putting all my eggs in one basket by any means.

```
┌─────────────────────────────┐
│          Olivier            │
│                             │
│  I love you. I'm desperate to │
│  hear your voice darling xxx  │
│                             │
│                             │
│                             │
│                             │
│  Options    Reply    Open    │
└─────────────────────────────┘
```

DECEMBER 7TH, 2004

It's been weeks since I wrote in this book. The longer I leave it the harder it gets because so much happens in between each time I get the chance.

I had three nights away with Olivier, which were fantastic, then flew back to Menorca with the girls, along with Tom, who was on the same flight for the weekend. Having not seen each other for nearly six weeks it was quite emotional. Since having witnessed his parent's behavior towards me, it made me feel quite sorry for him. My parents would never be so judgmental or biased towards me in any breakup of a relationship. I had more of an understanding where some of his behavior came from now.

We stood in a car park swapping over the kids, and had a big hug followed by quite a few tears out of sight of the girls. Tears for the years gone by, the love that we had once had and the love we would always have for sharing our beautiful daughters (even if we pretended to hate each other we would always have our eternal bond).

We spent some time together over that weekend that varied from cool and reasonable to typical horror story behavior. He shouted at me so loudly in the garden that Daisy and Amber begged him to stop from their bedroom window. He blamed me as always.

We spoke a little about Peru, which he wasn't interested in at all, then him—AGAIN.

Then he left for England.

That was nine days ago now. Since then I decided to go on a mission to get the house sorted and festive for the girls with a tree and decorations, and make it as comfortable as could be until Christmas at least.

I told both girls about Olivier a couple of days ago. I asked Daisy "How would you feel if I had a boyfriend?"

"I'd love it!" she said and so I decided to tell them about him and I. Both of them were so lovely, excited and strangely, not at all shocked.

"Can he dance?" was Amber's first question.

"If you get married can we be your bridesmaids?" was her second. When Tom tells me I'm ruining their lives forever I know I'm not. I'm changing it major style, I know, but who is he to judge what the future holds for us all?

He could end up happier with someone far more suitable for him than I ever was. As long as they wore green wellies, Alice bands, oversized polo tops with leggings and Gucci's, he'd be fine. The real 'mumsy' type was what he needed and whom he should have married from the start.

When I am with my girls without him, we are a tight team. We all get on. Everyone's happy. Everyone knows where we stand, routine and continuity. Peace. Tom seems to forget that we have spent a large proportion of our life here without him around anyway.

Olivier

Those beautiful daughters are so lucky to have such a talented, creative, special mother. I'm sure they are just like you! xxx

Options   Reply   Open

Olivier and I had a long chat last night about the possible future. Spain may be out of the question as a country we could live together in. Big decision time. It's Tuesday today and he's invited me to Helsinki on Thursday, so we will see what happens.

Anonymous

I saw you on the beach
walking today with your
girls and your dogs. What a
lovely sight to watch.

Options   Reply   Open

Meanwhile, I've been receiving anonymous texts from someone here on the island.
I know it's someone that knows me. Whoever it is has made Olivier very jealous which I
find quite funny. I'm not used to anyone getting jealous over me.

DECEMBER 8TH, 2004

```
Olivier

I'm very busy today my
darling with these clients.
We have non-stop
functions so I will call as
soon as I can but it won't
be until late. I love you.
Have a nice day xxx

Options     Reply     Open
```

We haven't been able to fix up where and when we are next going to see each other, and I'm cross with myself for feeling so obsessed. I'm fed up. Fed up of being here alone when all I want to do is be with him. It's been two weeks since we last were together and it feels like months. I want to see him while we're talking. I'm dying to cuddle him and can't wait to wake up in bed with him. I feel jealousy which I haven't felt for years.

I thought of him entertaining today, on sparkling form for drinks, parties, etc. I imagined all these beautiful, smart business women surrounding him like bees round a honey pot.

I hated it.

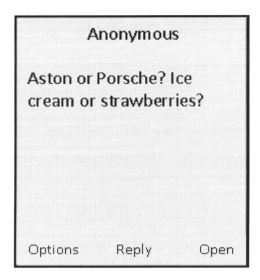

I wonder who that stranger could be? Being admired by someone else is quite bizarre as I'm not interested in anyone or anything else.

Where on earth are the girls and I going to be in six months' time? Why don't I have a fixed plan to work on?

I flew to London to meet Olivier for a surprise evening he had planned for us. I liked his surprises as they were always so imaginative and certainly I could never predict what we would be doing. I loved that. My flight was late so as per usual I had to change out of my flip-flops, shorts and T-shirt, into a sparkling dress and heels en route to the address he had given me. St John's, Smith Square SW1. I had no idea where I was going so as the cab pulled up I saw this vision standing on the steps surrounded by candle light lining the entrance.

He kissed me and took my hand to guide me in, as the performance was about to start... The Ambache chamber orchestra with a celebration of Mozart and the anniversary of Louise Farrenc. Wow. Wasn't expecting this at all. It was soooo grown up.

We sat straight down, barely having time to even say hello and held hands tightly. As the music started I watched his expressions and marveled at his creativeness to bring me to something like this.

I slowly reached into my handbag to get a pen to write a message on the program to him.

"Do you think anyone would notice if I sat on your lap? I'm so mad about you it's impossible to concentrate!"

He wrote back.

" Darling I would love you to sit on my lap, but I think some people would be upset...! You look stunning by the way and I can't wait to hold you against me."

" What time is your flight?

" I have to leave you at 6:15 a.m."

Great. Always land with a bump at those predictable words.

December 11th, 2004

Saturday lunch time and I'm feeling crap. It's raining and miserable.

Tom arrived yesterday and gave me the same lines over and over again.

"Why I am so intent on ruining everyone's lives."

When I spend time around him I feel so shattered, weak and emotional before, during and after being with him. I can't help the way I feel, the way I feel about the way we are together. Empty. I get all his tears and sadness, then major aggression. As soon as I see a softer side to him he blows it away with giving me such a hard time, it overrides any kindness or belief I could have in us again.

I will see Olivier again on Monday night, now he's got a flight with two unnecessary days in the London office booked in. Apparently his secretary thinks he's mad, as he has no work in London that needs him present. Here I am, sitting in the best kitchen I could imagine having. Original fireplace with the ancient, enormous chopping block that I'm writing at whilst I'm looking out of the windows over the gardens and pool, with the giant palm tree lit up in all its glory. My dream home. Paradise and I'm giving it all up.

```
┌─────────────────────────────────────┐
│                                      │
│          Anonymous                   │
│                                      │
│   Have you any idea who this         │
│   is?                                │
│                                      │
│                                      │
│                                      │
│                                      │
│                                      │
│                                      │
│                                      │
│   Options      Reply      Open       │
│                                      │
└─────────────────────────────────────┘
```

God, my life is crazy. I need to work out what the game plan for the next six months is. It's strange to think I can't remember ever feeling so like a canvas with no paint on it, a picture just about to be created. I have no idea even what it will be of? Maybe of two children, two dogs, two cats, and me? Have I got the courage to start a life in Barcelona? Alone, with not a soul I know?

It's a year next week that Olivier and I met. What a ridiculous year. The last six months even crazier than the first six months (with 15 guys on site here at the house everyday) No wonder I'm seven stone!

December 21st, 2004

I'm on my knees. It is unquestionably so much harder being completely alone when it comes to running this huge household of kids and animals, whilst also singlehandedly taking care of all the gardens and mowing all the lawns, so a lot of what I feel is pure exhaustion. All the workmen have gone months ago but this is all part of what I've created.

Three Christmas cards. Not the usual three hundred. We don't even get post here anyway, along with a loose DVD of the movie 'Unfaithful' left for me by Tom. Nice.

(One huge benefit of leaving him is that I NEVER will have to suffer one of his ghastly sister's, and I mean hideous, Christmases ever again). She truly was my idea of hell on legs. HOORAY!!!!

I can't wait to spend some time with some friends. People that love me, and who I love being with. I'm so looking forward to being with my two best mates, in particular Jules and Sally. All the craziness, all the banter, all the laughs and the familiarity we have.

Daisy keeps asking about Olivier now. She asked me yesterday,

"If you marry him would you have another baby? When will I meet Olivier? You know mummy the most important thing is he loves you." Incredible words from a six year old.

December 22nd, 2004

When I feel down, depressed, lonely, bored, which I've felt a lot of over the last week I know it's mainly because I'm missing Olivier more than I ever have. Several people have made a comment that completely freaks me out; Swiss men are renowned for never leaving their wives. They have love affairs as often as hot breakfasts. It is commonplace and the wives tend to accept it. Jesus Christ, I HATE hearing that.

Part of me keeps thinking, be serious—does he really love you enough to leave all of it for me? And if I end up made a fool of, loving him and it was never going to happen because he'd never leave his wife, then I will be wiser for it and I would obviously have to try and accept it. But I can't imagine that because I don't want to imagine it right now. Maybe he is in my life to teach me a big lesson?

Every time I get a message I just light up. Every time we talk my heart races.

It's not getting any easier to cope with. I feel like I'm going into Christmas on my knees though. We won't see each other until the 29th.

JANUARY 4TH, 2005

Olivier may have left me. Forever. I know he is so torn and in so much pain. He can't find a solution in order to be with me. Christmas for him was with his wife and girls, followed by two days with me before we parted on New Year's Eve, before he went back to work.

I think I cried from the minute we arrived at the restaurant until we left. And I woke up crying as he left in the morning. He cried too. It was absolutely heartbreaking. Of course I can't accept it's over because I love him so much. I couldn't imagine being without him in my life.

It's been four days since we had contact. The message I got last night made me feel a little better. He's still thinking about me. I will wait as long as I need to for him. If what we have is what he wants, he won't be able to continue this way. He has already separated from her before so I'm sure he can do it again, but maybe next time not for me.

The only peace I have at the moment is that he is suffering too.

JANUARY 5TH, 2005

It's another beautiful day here. The sky is so blue and the sun is warm. It's good to be alive today.

I have a strange feeling reading that, I don't know what to make of it. We haven't actually spoken since New Year's Eve. He's calling me at 4 p.m. today. If we know it could never be then surely we wouldn't be suffering so much? Whatever the reason I'm not letting go or giving up yet. I told Olivier on the phone tonight that talk is cheap.

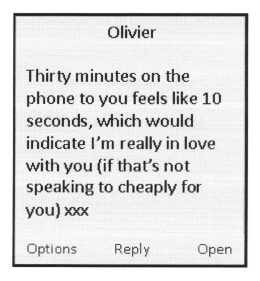

JANUARY 10TH, 2005

Another few days of highs and lows. Tom calling from the Alps saying he was going to jump, making me feel sick with worry. Yesterday I kept thinking that I wished I could help him through his pain. There are so many things he has to get his head around for himself that I just can't help him with. Emotional guilt trips are his specialty at the moment, telling me consistently that I'm going to regret this forever. Was I sure I knew what I was doing? I just wish he could get through the barrier and realize that yes, life is going to be different. No, he hasn't lost his girls. He's just lost me as his wife.

He wants to go back to how we were, and I don't. I've seen there's another life out there and I don't want to go back to what has been. I couldn't now even if I wanted to. (I found out later that he wasn't on a mountaintop about to jump. He was on the balcony of a chalet with some girl under the duvet he'd taken away for the weekend, waiting for him to come back to bed. He is SO full of shit.)

```
┌─────────────────────────────┐
│          Olivier            │
│                             │
│ Whatever happens            │
│ between us I swear I have    │
│ never loved anyone like I   │
│ love you. I'm not giving up  │
│ darling. xxx                │
│                             │
│                             │
│                             │
│  Options    Reply    Open   │
└─────────────────────────────┘
```

Today was an interesting day in many ways. I went to sleep after that beautiful message from Olivier and when we spoke early this morning I dived straight into him when he called me. We must have talked for at least two hours today along with fifty messages at least. Ridiculous really.

This evening Tom has rung here at least fifty times. Each time having no regard whatsoever as to what I'm doing, whether I'm washing the girls' hair, making them supper, or sitting down to watch TV (which I never do) for the first time in months.

He just kept on ringing again and again on the landline and my mobile.

"What about me, here by myself…me, me, me, poor me, but you're screwed up, you're a family breaker, etc., etc., etc. Don't you care about me, eating my dinner alone?"

All the same lines I've been hearing for so many months now.

I'm so in love, I know how that feels now so how could I ever, ever, give that up and go back to what?

JAN 12TH, 2005

Another bizarre day, but I feel a bit less scared about the future and whether Olivier will have the courage to start a new life with me. I can feel he is trying to resist less than before.

I'm so tired. I just wish I could sleep for a week. This is by far the most exhausting of all emotions. I hope in the next month or two I can work on getting this house finished and ready to be on the market by April. I'm going to start painting the kitchen tomorrow.

JANUARY 13TH, 2005

Tom's coming in the morning, so I'm trying to not worry about it tonight. The sooner we agree on some kind of settlement the better, and then we can have a relationship that has no holds over each other. His bullying, controlling, obsessive behavior drives me further and further away. I'm obviously supposed to be where I am. And in fact as he keeps pushing me, I get further and further to a place in my mind where he can't get me. Remember, everything happens for a reason.

```
┌─────────────────────────────┐
│          Olivier            │
│                             │
│  I couldn't think about you │
│  more than I do. You occupy │
│  every thought I have all the│
│  time. I can't wait to see  │
│  you! I can't wait! Xxx I   │
│  hope you will still like me...│
│                             │
│  Options    Reply    Open   │
└─────────────────────────────┘
```

Olivier told me today that I had taken his heart and maybe his soul. He also told me not to drink too much tonight as I've been invited out to a party. No one has ever said anything like that to me without me being made to feel bad. I liked it. I liked the fact that he cared and the fact is, he's probably right. I spend nearly every night alone once the girls are in bed, at the kitchen island with my book, my candles, my music and the best part of a bottle of wine to myself whilst I write this diary.

Mind you if he actually could see what goes on in my life hourly at the moment he would probably think it's a miracle that I'm not a raving alcoholic!

February 4th, 2005

Can't believe it's been weeks since I wrote. Every time I've thought of it, it's too much to remember to write down. I've been to Nice for the weekend. Barcelona for the weekend and London too since last I wrote in this diary. Quite a few weeks! Olivier rang the night before Tom arrived for a weekend with the girls, to ask me to fly down to the south of France to meet him for the night. We had a great time until I had my handbag from the hire car stolen whilst we were walking on the beach. Passport, cash, cards, Spanish and UK phones, MY LIFE! I was stranded in Nice. He had already boarded his flight back to Geneva as I went to get mine when I was told I couldn't fly without my passport! Brilliant.

I sat there in the Nice airport with my head in my hands, having no idea what I was going to do. An hour later, still panicking, I watched a woman coming towards me saying that my husband was on the phone for me at her desk. MY HUSBAND?? Jesus, how the hell did he know that I was there? In fact it wasn't him but Olivier who just wanted to check I'd got on the plane OK! THANK GOD. He saved my ass with organizing a hotel and cash for me. I was desperate. Totally stripped of my identity, but I got a new passport the next day. I got back to the island eventually on Sunday and like a bad, scolded child I had to deal obviously with a livid Tom (who had thought I was somewhere else on the island) for an hour or so until he flew off back to London.

We went to court on Thursday for the start of our divorce proceedings as he has gone behind my back wanting to divorce here rather than in the UK. Probably because the average woman here in the village survives on six Euros a week in their flats, bakes their own bread, knits her own underwear and milks the cow for cereal milk for the children every morning. Great, he is going to try and screw me over then.

I'm now in bed. It's Friday night and its 10:30 p.m. I've had a long hot bath but I still feel miserable. How did I get here? I wish I could turn the clock back a few years. I hope I'm not making a huge mistake. I hate being lonely. I hate sleeping by myself night after night. I miss a lot of people, many of my friends. I'm fed up with the lows on the roller coaster ride of my life. I couldn't get hold of Olivier, who had been flying to USA whilst I was asleep.

The old me rather before I feel in love with you. I'm afraid to even say those words because of what it implies. Before I wished that I didn't think of you day and night now that's all I do. I don't deserve your love as I have made

Options   Reply   Open

You wait too long..
Hope you are ok. Night darling xxx

Options   Reply   Open

FEBRUARY 18TH, 2005

Again it's been weeks since I've found or made time to write in this. What's happening?

I need to get some good advice this week. Tom and I have to reach a decision about finances ASAP. I need to finish Bona Ventura myself if he refuses to help me.

I want to be separated financially.

Olivier

I'm madly in love with you
darling and will do
whatever it takes to be
with you xxx

Options   Reply   Open

It's been nearly three weeks since I've seen Olivier but it feels like forever. I swore I couldn't do that kind of torture again. But I have and I've got through it. I'm now climbing the walls. I wonder how I will feel again. I always partially prepare myself for him to be different, but I think he will be as wonderful as ever, gorgeous. I woke up about a hundred times in the night, like I usually do. When I watch him get dressed in the mornings I do have to pinch myself. Yum yum. The night only seems to include no more than two hours at a time of proper sleep. He makes me laugh so much, too.

God knows how he operates in the office after seeing me!

I look a lot better than I have in months, even years maybe? I've had loads of sleep and not too much booze, plus I've been eating well and it shows. I feel good.

FEBRUARY 21ST, 2005

Daisy's birthday today! I came back up to London with Kristy, my other closest girlfriend and her husband Ralph to meet Olivier for dinner in Chelsea later that evening. He gave me a painting for Valentine's Day. Two arum lilies. I don't think I have ever been given a gift so thoughtful. He knew it was my favorite flower and that I had planted hundreds in the garden in Spain. I gave him a pair of cufflinks I'd had engraved from Tiffany's. One said 'WANT' the other said 'NEED'.

I'm seeing Viv this afternoon, which I hope will help give me a boost of strength to keep my armor intact. I'm going to really miss the girls this week. Hate being apart from them.

MARCH 2ND, 2005

Well, I'm back at home with the girls after my ten days in London. When Tom and I had met at the airport we had ten minutes of tears with a strange cuddle. I rushed back so excited to see the girls that we all danced and danced in the kitchen together. Upstairs, my bedroom had been redecorated with ripped-up service sheets from our wedding and photos, along with a horrible letter from him, which I quickly cleared up before the girls saw them.

Daisy had made me a card, which said:

Mummy

Daisy and Amber love you so much

So happy you're home again

Love Daisy

xxxxxxxxxx

I cried behind my smiles for them, feeling terrible. So tired, emotionally ruined, and I still feel the same five days later.

```
┌─────────────────────────────┐
│          Olivier            │
│                             │
│  I don't think I have the   │
│  strength you need me to    │
│  have for you darling. I'm a│
│  wreck xxx                  │
│                             │
│                             │
│                             │
│  Options    Reply     Open  │
└─────────────────────────────┘
```

MARCH 5TH, 2005

It's been ten months now since I started the affair with Olivier. Tom and I go to court next Friday, then it's all over. I feel I have no strength. I feel so low, lost, alone, confused and completely empty. Olivier has told me again that he hasn't got the strength to start a new life with me. I know he's feeling desperate and so am I. It's been three days of virtually no contact, which is killing me. I really need him, especially right now. I can't really write. I feel so weak. I can't believe where I am. Can't believe it's all happening and I don't want it to stop, even though it's all so painful. I have absolutely no idea whatsoever where I am going.

Tom said today that where I'm going the grass wouldn't be greener. It will be short and brown. My father told me on the phone tonight, "Don't wait for your boat to come in, row out to meet it." "I'm going to, just you watch, even if I have to fly with no wings!" I replied, at the same time as trying to convince myself.

MARCH 6TH, 2005

It's Tom's 40th birthday. I'm feeling much better today. Even though it's raining and cold and I'm alone with the girls in my gilded cage, losing power every few hours in the middle of nowhere, I'm OK. I'm alive. I lay awake for hours last night thinking, thinking, and thinking, with the duvet tightly cocooning me in the cold, complete darkness and silence.

My sister Hannah reminded me on the phone earlier, from Australia, that one day she remembered once I was so run down but I'd still got up, got dressed up and went and kicked ass at some meeting, scoring a great interiors deal. I've got to get through this week and I WILL. I have to stop being afraid of my future. I have the courage; I've got this far. I just need to keep on remembering that Tom is not good for me! AT ALL!

My beautiful, lovely, charming, peaceful, soul mate Olivier seems to have abandoned me again just when I need him the most. How could he? By going silent on me like this now he is forcing me to be even stronger in myself without having his love and support at the worst time in my life.

Olivier

Have you heard of
asymmetry? It's when
someone (me) is more
likely to be dumped than
someone else (you). It
drives me mad FYI xxx

Options   Reply   Open

It's Mother's Day today!

Yippee. Don't I feel like the perfect mother?! I've spoken to Olivier. He still loves me and I haven't lost him, so funnily enough I feel able to cope again, in my pathetic way. I don't care that I'm dependent on him at the moment. He gives me such strength and self-belief, so if that's a bad thing, then tough.

Tom's been calling again, again and again. With all the phones consistently ringing all evening in this house I have to walk outside rather than unplug them all. Every time I do speak to him I go cold. He says the same every time: "Look what you've done, do you really want a divorce? Do you really know what you are doing, throwing away a good man? You're throwing away your family and the girls' future."

I go and file my nails furiously trying to think of something else. The phone stops after a while. The music plays, I smoke cigarettes, I go and have a long hot bath and I go to bed. Tomorrow is another day, another Monday, a new week ahead. I'll get through it and if I can see Olivier then I'll get through it a lot easier.

The bloody generator is going off all the time so it's absolutely freezing in Amityville!

I'm unplugging heaters every time I want to cook. And God forbid I should need to cook after heating the hot water tanks for a bath for the girls. I read a quote today, which stuck in my mind:

"We must be willing to get rid of the life we have planned, so as to have the life that is waiting for us."

—Joseph Campbell

Olivier

Darling why won't you
answer your phone?

Options   Reply   Open

Olivier

It seems I am at the
bottom of your priorities
now?

Options   Reply   Open

Olivier

We aren't married yet but
there is definitely potential
as we are already arguing
over nothing! xxx

Options   Reply   Open

MARCH 7TH, 2005

I hardly slept last night. I was in bed at 10:30 and think I was still awake around 2 a.m. Could barely move at 7:20 when I got the girls up but I'm feeling a little stronger on my own two feet. Olivier and I are back on track again because I initiated communication. Thank god. We both realized it was a misunderstanding. He has to realize that whilst he sits in his mansion on the lake in Geneva, I'm sometimes sitting in the dark and freezing cold, trying to keep the girls and my spirits up. I'm not always available to have a 'nice chat' whilst I'm boiling kettles for a bath for them, trying to do homework too whilst scrubbing floors, cooking, walking dogs and maintaining the grounds.

He told me tonight he was taking sixty-hour Spanish lessons in case I stayed in Spain.

He says he hopes I haven't given up on him. Of course I haven't. Why would I?

My father said to me on the phone tonight that maybe Olivier was like an angel sent to guide me through these times. I will be eternally grateful for having ever had him in my life, for however long he will stay with me. Yes, he's more serious than me by far.

Yes, he's ten million times more intelligent. Yes, he doesn't laugh or smile as much as he could.

Yes, he's the most beautiful man I've ever kissed. Yes, he's the most interesting. And yes, he's the best thing that's happened to me in a very long time.

MARCH 9TH, 2005

All the phones rang nonstop last night. I knew exactly who it was so I didn't take the calls. I surrendered only to a few glasses of wine and slept very deeply for a change.

I'd like to be a writer one day. I've decided that I can see myself banging away on a computer or writing in a book day after day. I like the idea of being in a lovely space, lots of light, music, either painting or writing. I wonder if I will ever make that happen.

I hope so. You have to keep on dreaming, hey?

MARCH 16TH, 2005

I've been numb for the past week. We went to court on Friday for a three hour ordeal. Hideous. My father flew out and held my hand all the way to the court as I hardly slept three nights prior to it. So pleased to get that hug from him I needed so badly.

Ironically, Tom had his friend, Adam flown in for the occasion. The most sickening, insipid, philandering, predatory misogynist of a human being standing giving evidence against me. For what? MY adultery?

It was a joke. The guy is a world-class wanker. He makes a fortune out of screwing people over through insurance claims, so screwing me over was a walk in the park for him. He stood there in his slippery, deceitful way telling the judge that I didn't earn us any money. Tom told the judge that my work on our houses was "just the gravy on a dish that he made." Well, sod you both. Ten years of designing, marketing, dressing and selling all our properties, having put my heart and soul into every single one I'd done, and I was just 'gravy'?

In the morning when Tom brought the girls home to me having had them for the night in our apartment on the port, I felt very emotional with the reality of what was happening. We hugged then cried for ten minutes, before he left to fly back with Adam 'the worm' sitting smugly in his front passenger seat.

My father had left an hour before, so suddenly I was alone again. Everyone was calling, texting to see how I was. I couldn't talk to anyone. I think even Tom felt guilty for being so dishonest, having lowered himself to that level against me. I still haven't five days later. My mind has been so confused I haven't wanted to burden and confuse loved ones even more than I have already.

Olivier

Darling, take care of
yourself please. Many
people need you and rely
on you. Many think you are
a great, generous, lively,
clever, strong and dynamic
woman. You give to others

Options   Reply   Open

Sometimes without you
even knowing and you may
not always be repaid. Keep
going darling but think
about yourself a little
more. The way you lives
enchants me and puzzles
me. I swear you are like no
one I've ever met before.

Options   Reply   Open

You are amazing. I wish
this wasn't so hard on you
but I'm not giving up. I
hope you find some peace
in the coming days ahead.
When can we speak? xxx

Options   Reply   Open

Tom said to me last night "If I was prepared to take you back, if I was to forgive your

hideous affair..." What the hell is he talking about? I left HIM. It would be me coming

back, hopefully meeting him halfway, if I was ever going to want to. I'm so confused.

I can't believe I've been having doubts so late in the day at the 12th hour. I can't move

to Barcelona. I think I'm going to have to take the girls back to England. I have to look at

the options in a new light. I have to separate myself from the climate, lifestyle and outdoor living. That's very, very hard to do. I have to think about Daisy and Amber's schooling, friends in the UK, the support network, social life, grandparents, etc, etc they would still be able to see their friends here when they come back with Tom and his parents.

"It's always darkest before the dawn," my dear friend Emma said to me yesterday.

When the light comes in I want to be flooded in it. I want to roll around in its warmth. I'm ever the optimist. Self respect? I have it. I stick to my path, follow my dream. Believe in myself. "I believe in days ahead, don't spend another night alone wishing you were dead" is playing on the radio by Scissor Sisters. I sang it at the top of my voice in the garden as I picked flowers for the kitchen. The hardest thing to do is break the dependency, pushing through the pain headfirst.

The struggle.

The helplessness.

The loneliness.

The confusion.

Will it eventually pass?

MARCH 18TH, 2005

State of independence. It is such a glorious day today, so sunny and warm. Crystal blue skies. It's good to be waking up before my alarm, with the sun pouring in from the bathroom window from the east, through onto my heavenly bed.

I've been thinking more and more about London. Keep seeing myself at my computer in a room with really high ceilings and big windows. Even if it's only grey sky outside. I'm not deluding myself about that. It's a very large part of this whole decision leaving Spain.

The beautiful country I love so much, with the outdoor life, with the sunshine, the people, the food, and the sea. I have to keep reminding myself it's not forever. What I do now and what I do in two years time could be two very different things.

MARCH 21ST, 2005

Right, I'm ready to get on now, really ready. No plans seem forthcoming from the opposition, so once again I think it will have to be me that pushes ahead with the proposals.

Maybe Tom thinks I will just end up rotting here, losing hope the longer he leaves this. "I'm prepared to forgive you and your affair."

What is he on? After months upon months of saying the same thing, my message is still falling on deaf ears: "I don't want us to be together anymore. I'm sorry but I'm happier without you and we don't have a future. I'm sorry I've shattered your dream and ruined your life, but I can't come back because I don't want to." Black and white again, again, again. Saying it the first time was the hardest thing I've ever had to say, so I wish he would listen to me for once in his life.

When I read that I thought, well, swap lives with me for a day. That's TORTURE!

MARCH 22ND, 2005

I'm in darkness again. No bloody fuel again. Silence engulfs the house. Girls are painting in candlelight in the kitchen, totally engrossed. I don't even have power to call for anyone to help. All batteries are dead. Keep on smiling. Tom told me that if I leave the island to see Olivier when he is here this weekend then I would have war on my hands.

When will he realize he's fighting the mother of his children? Hurting me consistently trying to get at me, will only hurt them. I'm their mother, for god's sake.

Will you ever just give me a break? Ever?

Memo to myself: Remember to focus on the good.

I read another lovely quote today:

"Find a place inside where there's joy and the joy will burn out the pain."

MARCH 26TH, 2005

We have to go to court again on Thursday. Do his parents know?

Olivier

Whatever happens with us
I want you to be happy. It
hurts me to think that I
make you feel indifferent
xxx

Options   Reply   Open

April 27th, 2005

Thirty-two days since I last wrote this. I don't know what happened. I've been here, there, back over there, here again, away again and now I'm back in the kitchen alone.

No closer whatsoever to knowing where I'm going next.

No one can help me. No one can tell me what the right thing is to do. I haven't spoken to anyone for two weeks because I don't know what to say.

I delayed the divorce for a month to try and talk to Tom, to spend time together as he was being reasonable for the first time in a very long time, completely throwing me off my course because a part of me still loves him. I just have absolutely no idea what I'm going to do. My mind goes from one extreme to the other within minutes. Do I stay with Tom after all? After all this? Leave him? How do I make the right decisions? How do I get to the point when I know what I'm doing and am completely and utterly sure? Do I stick to my plan to move back to London, to get on with my career, get the girls into a good school and leave Spain? Leave Tom? Leave the most beautiful home in the world with this idyllic life the girls love? I know I am going to, so what am I most scared of? I walked down the straight mile-long drive to the house this afternoon in the hot sunshine with the dogs. I looked at the barley, which has now grown to five foot tall, stunning fields upon fields of gold. All the heads were swaying this way, then that way, changing direction in seconds in the warm breeze. It's like my mind, I thought: waves of thought, emotion and feeling.

I just walked into the living room with all my candles flickering, the music playing, and our beautiful home. Our beautiful Bona Ventura. The dogs are in their chair on top of each other. They couldn't be happier. What I can't seem to work out is if I was happy before, then what happened? How did I let it go so far? Is it me? Could I be happy again with my life as it was with Tom, our family together under one roof? What is it that is missing that is so noticeable to me? Can't I just pretend to be happy?

What really does make me happy? What is going on? Am I ever going to be complete? What's stopping me from embracing my future? I'm so scared. The longer this goes on the more lost I feel.

SEPTEMBER 26TH, 2005

Where have I been, and what the hell has been going on for the past, oh my god it's been the last 5 months? As I was just cleaning my manor house utility room (the size of a small football field) for the first and the last time today, I thought that was a good time to pick this up and write again.

I'm leaving everything I have here in the morning. My parents were on the phone tonight helping me through my painful last hours here in this life, which is over.

"Is your car facing the house, as usual?" Katie asked me.

"Yes."

"Well go out there now and turn it around to face the right direction, the way you are headed," she said. I walked out into the garden for a final reflection in the silence of the night, with just the moon and stars above me with the crickets buzzing. This is it.

This is the end of this life, and in six hours time I will be on my way to the next one.

I tucked my dogs into bed for the last time, more heartbreaking than anything. I sat down in their basket with them hugging them, stroking their faces, wiping away the tears, which were falling fast and furiously.

"You are hardest to leave. I never wanted to leave you in a million years. If I could make it happen you would be in that car coming with me," I whispered to them, wishing they could understand my words.

I'd had Dolly ever since I was pregnant with Daisy. She had been my best friend ever since. She was one in a million. I had lost count of the days she and I would go on walks when I needed to cry out of sight from the girls, all the times she saved me.

With a paw on my lap, she would look up at me with her big brown eyes, full of love and loyalty. She always made me feel better, like she could feel my pain. But I had to leave her behind with Tom now. with her daughter Chica. By the time they woke up I would be in mainland Spain.

Destination—new life in London.

NOVEMBER 11TH, 2005

My father's birthday today so I will try and sound strong, like I'm coping, on the phone for him. I'm still in a dark place but I'm back in London town. I just don't know where to start filling in the huge gaps over the past 6 months.

I went back to Tom—there, I said it. I still can't believe I did. I was on my knees, an emotional and physical wreck with no direction. I found myself crying and hugging him. WHAT THE HELL WAS I THINKING? Maybe I was thinking, just maybe, we could get over what had happened, so the only way to see if we could was to try yet again.

I told him that he should come to stay at the house to see how we got on.

I tried to be prepared for the challenges we had ahead of us. Mountains we had to climb together, so many difficult conversations, with explaining to do on both sides, in order to work out how our marriage got to this point. How the hell did I became so unhappy that I looked for love elsewhere?

On the first evening we spent together, I took the time to make myself look as good as I could before he arrived. I did my hair the way he liked it, and as I put makeup on I felt like I was getting ready for an unprecedented scenario. I had hope, as much as I could have, anyway. One of the only benefits of living in 'Amityville' was I'd given a bed in one of the guest rooms and bathroom in its own domain, to a homeless chef for three months, in return for teaching me how to cook like Nigella Lawson. Tom didn't know that I was now a real master in the kitchen! Dinner was the only part of the evening ahead I wasn't worrying about.

When we sat down, after we had wandered around the garden, the very first words to leave Tom's lips were, "I hope you know that it's you that has a lot, a lot, of making up to do. You have hurt so many people with your hideous behavior. There are a lot of people who will need to forgive you. You have lots of sorries to say to a lot of people. You have a lot more work to do rebuilding this marriage than I have. You need to realize that now."

That was it. Those words confirmed that we would never ever be together again. I knew it for sure then. There would never be a time we would connect again. Whatever love we had was gone. We truly couldn't be more strangers if we tried.

I said very little. I just stared at the delicious dinner I had made with no appetite, realizing that I really was flogging a very dead horse. I was completely lying to myself. How could I? Then, after what he'd said, I could only think of Olivier and how I hated it every second without him in my life. He didn't make me feel anything that Tom did all the time. He made me feel love not just crap about myself and who I am.

Olivier

I know I'm not funny and too quiet at times bit I can only improve as the woman I love is very stimulating and so lovely! xxx

Options   Reply   Open

I sit here now nearly six months later looking back, totally amazed by myself!! I got my car back eventually, paid for. I concentrated on finishing the house and marketing it.

I tried to come to terms with the fact that Olivier probably wouldn't ever leave his wife and I just existed. We had my birthday party at the house and enjoyed everyone's company other than each other's as Tom made jokes with all our guests at my expense, trying to appear the 'good man' for giving me another chance, after "everything I'd done to him." How kind. Pretending was a complete deception. Too late, too far from where we once started. We had gone so far I couldn't even see where we'd come from, where we had once started out. I couldn't go near him. I loathed him with the recent memories of all he'd put me through to punish me.

Game over.

In my brain it was like going down to the end of my imaginary garden, finding the biggest, heaviest log I could find, dragging it back to the house, and beating myself with it. I had to go there though, in every sense of the word. I thought my father would be furious with me when I told him, but I couldn't have been more wrong. He told me that he admired me for having the courage once again to try to seek the truth. He was proud of me for trying again for the girls' sake and for me to finally be able to close the book. If I hadn't tried, I wouldn't know. The truth was it was the end of the road and it was a dead end for sure.

Bona Ventura was sold two months later to a sweet couple from Madrid, having been made as beautiful as I could with no funds and more sweat and stress than I care to remember. Good luck to them with their 'good adventure!'…

Tom and I split the value of all our furniture which the couple had bought, and I left Spain and with one loaded car. I took the ferry over to the main land, and headed to Barcelona to meet Fi, my new girlfriend, whom I had met that summer from England. She was up for a 'Thelma and Louise' journey. She was such fun with a great energy about her. Feisty and very entertaining. I left with a mere 15,000 euros after 8 years of marriage. Basically enough to put down a deposit at the school and two months' rent—that's it. That was what I had to start a new life for the girls and me.

Checked into Hotel Arts, one of my favorite hotels in the world, with a late booking deal. I put the cash in their main safe and lost the key within an hour, whereupon I was told by a snotty receptionist that it would cost between three to four thousand euros to blowtorch it open I drank champagne like it was going out of fashion to celebrate my newfound freedom (courtesy of the manager, who was lurking around us), left the next day having had the main safe opened for me (for free, much to the receptionist's disgust!) and headed up through Spain into France with the roof off, drinking Red Bulls, playing music at top volume all the way back to the King's Road, Chelsea, London.

I wonder now if I could have seen what I was going to have to go though in order to be away from him, whether I would have had the guts.

It's really killed me and I'm far from out of the woods. In fact from where I'm sitting, these woods still look very deep and very dark.

My phone screen saver is our pool at Bona Ventura, which I designed; it now feels like years ago. This is like a bad dream. I cannot believe that Tom has coincidentally decided to go bust now and not give me a bean to provide anything.

How the hell does he expect me to support our girls?

Fi came over with a pizza and a bottle of bubbly, and now I'm sitting alone, my candles are burning, my music is playing, and I'm feeling desperate. Wish someone could say a word or two to me to brighten the dark. The most important thing is that the girls are really loving their school and making lots of friends so that's one box ticked. 3654 to go. When will pleasure beat the pain?

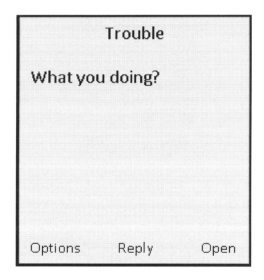

Why does this guy, who I randomly met on my first night back in London, keep texting me? He was all over me like a cheap suit that night; I couldn't get rid of him! So annoying, wish I hadn't given him my number. He is a developer, so he was implying we could do some work together. I put him in my phone under Trouble, but should change it to Pain in the Ass instead. He unloaded on me all about how his girlfriend, whom he had left, had fallen pregnant; he didn't love her but was deeply confused. I needed to hear his issues like

I needed to shoot myself in the face. No offence but I was maxing out with my own shit. This was the first night of my 'new' life, but thank you anyway for sharing…

Olivier

I don't want you to ever replace me. We are made for each other xxx

Options   Reply   Open

November 23rd, 2005

Sod folding the washing in my hutch corridor at 10:30 at night. I have had such a breakthrough that I had to make a point of stopping to find a pen (hard to do in this house) and a chair to reach this book from the top of my wardrobe. It's my home and I still hide it. What would a psychologist say about that I wonder?

In many ways it all feels like a lifetime ago that I was fighting to free myself, yet it's only been a matter of months. So much I never expected. So much I never considered, so much pain in saying goodbye to so much that was familiar, yet it never stopped me pressing on relentlessly. I never thought Tom would stitch me up like a kipper financially like this either. Never in a million years. Just shows how wrong you can be.

It must mean I have faith in myself? Either that or I'm just a glutton for life and the unexpected.

```
┌─────────────────────────────────┐
│             Trouble             │
│                                 │
│   We are having drinks on       │
│   the river if you would like   │
│   to join? Please answer??      │
│                                 │
│                                 │
│                                 │
│                                 │
│                                 │
│  Options      Reply      Open   │
└─────────────────────────────────┘
```

So here I am, surviving, would you believe it? I'm in my second month of being back in London town. Just me and my babies in our own home. Our 'mouse house,' which consists of three floors of Victorian terrace in Battersea, south London. Four flights of steep stairs with small rabbit-hutch rooms off the narrow hallways, two stunning big bathrooms with free-standing baths. A skinny but kind of cool flagstone-floored kitchen with the selling point being a fantastic eight-hob Smeg oven with vintage-style fridge.

Two open fires in the tiny living room with stripped wood floors into the dining room.

A small back yard with no more than four foot of flowerbeds, horrific rent but it's a perfect place for us to land back in London. Couldn't be more opposite to Bona Ventura, but it's sweet. I was in a real rush to get somewhere as soon as I had managed to get both the girls into one of the best private schools in London less than a mile away. All the other properties I saw on my brief, hectic home-finding trips to London looked awful. Really student-like, done on a strict budget with no style or taste. Plastic loo seats? I don't think so. I couldn't see us in any available house to rent here other than this one, so I took it.

```
┌─────────────────────────────┐
│                             │
│          Trouble            │
│                             │
│  So want to see you again...│
│                             │
│                             │
│                             │
│                             │
│                             │
│                             │
│                             │
│                             │
│                             │
│ Options    Reply      Open  │
└─────────────────────────────┘
```

I made a decision today, as it is Tom's turn to have the girls this year, so I booked a flight to Bangkok to see Andre and his great girlfriend Jodie for Christmas and New Year's.

They both had such positive outlooks on life and are a great tonic to go and hang out with. Nine whole days away in the sunshine, with friends and nothing else. A perfect opportunity to finally find the time to write this book and fill in the past five months.

I'm off to NYC on Friday too with Olivier for my weekend off. I think I have feathered the nest, as well as settled us all in enough to be able to go have a weekend away to myself.

December 11th, 2005

My trip to NYC wasn't quite what I had hoped for. It started off like a dream. I flew to Paris to meet him at the Virgin upper class desk in Charles de Gaulle.

When he arrived I was sitting, having breezed through, by bullshitting who I was, sipping a glass of champagne whilst online looking at restaurants in NYC. Ha! We had the very best seats on the plane, the two right at the very front with no one either side of you with the only interruption being having your glass of champagne refilled, or the question of how you would like your steak cooked tonight. I loved it. I was like a child, I was so entertained by all the gadgets and buttons. There was no way I was going to sleep in Upper Class! What a waste. This was the only way to travel, surely?

Turning left on the plane, not right, was the way to go.

Olivier enjoyed the novelty of my delight before he slipped into a full bed position, thinking he could sneak forty winks a couple of hours into the flight under the duvet. I pressed the wrong button, the one controlling his bed, and unable to reverse the change I watched him being put in the upright position again, much to his annoyance!

We checked into our hotel and headed straight out to the MOMA exhibition, which I've always wanted to see. Fascinating, inspiring and I loved every second in there. Afterwards we headed to Soho for a wander-around to shop. It was so bitterly cold I spent the entire time with an enormous cream fur hat fixed to my head, which covered my ears. It was a brilliant

hat. I had no idea that I would want to burn it by the time I arrived back to London, as it

started the biggest row we have had. By lunchtime maybe half a dozen different people had

stopped me on the street to ask where I had acquired it.

```
┌─────────────────────────────────┐
│                                 │
│          Trouble                │
│                                 │
│  Where are you? You never       │
│  answer your phone to me        │
│  – Are you abroad?              │
│                                 │
│                                 │
│                                 │
│                                 │
│  Options      Reply      Open   │
│                                 │
└─────────────────────────────────┘
```

We stopped for lunch in a busy little cafe full of people and atmosphere. Outside there

were market stalls selling their wares and when I stepped outside to smoke a cigarette I

watched an old English guy trying to sell stunning silver jewelry he had designed from the

veins on the backs of leaves. He was freezing cold, hungry, unshaven, and penniless but

with the biggest, brightest smile on his face. I admired his work, chatted for a few moments

about his home now being NYC, and how he wished he could afford to get back to surprise

his family back in the UK one Christmas.

I wanted to give him something but didn't need any of his jewelry in return. Before I

rejoined Olivier, I slipped the man the single $20 note that was in my jeans pocket, telling

to him to buy a Christmas drink on me later on. I wished him all the best for the New Year

and went back into the warmth inside.

We ate our lunch and just as we were about to get up to leave the jewelry maker walked into the busy restaurant searching around for somebody. I prayed he wasn't coming to see me as my hat had already attracted many unappreciated comments that had put Olivier's back up. He didn't like me getting attention. Sure enough as soon as the man spotted me, he approached our table holding one of his necklaces in a pretty blue box out to me. "I hope you don't mind but I wanted you to have this. You are very kind; I want you to keep this."

"Thank you very much, you didn't need to," I said slightly uncomfortable in the way Olivier was looking at me across the table. He paused as he left and turned to Olivier. "You're a lucky man sir; you have a lovely lady here."

Nothing more was mentioned about it until later that evening as we finished dinner headed for the club Crowbar. The second we walked in, two gay guys bowed to my hat: "Divine. Divine, sweetie!" I pretended I didn't hear them as I walked on by, my hand firmly in Olivier's. However stupid it was, he was pissed off and I knew it.

As we left, he went to the men's room as I went to get our coats from the cloakroom.

A young guy just arriving with his friend smiled at me. "Hello," he said. "Hello and goodbye," I replied, not even making eye contact, at exactly the same moment Olivier's fist came out of nowhere—hitting the stranger in the jaw so hard he was laid to the floor in one punch. Jesus Christ! The next thing I knew my hand is pressing hard into the chest of an eight foot bouncer heavier than 'Giant Hay Stacks' who is trying to get past me to chase after Olivier who was casually walking out seething.

I was frantically trying to do damage limitations, putting my other hand on this poor guy's arm saying "I'm so sorry, I don't know what the problem is with him, I'm so sorry, please don't get him." I don't know how, but I managed through straight talking to keep the 400lb pit bulls off Olivier as I rushed him into a waiting taxi jumping in at the last second as it sped away.

Idiot! I don't want a man like you, I thought, my heart racing so fast with fear. I hate violence with a passion. We are in NYC for fuck sake, not Ascot—anything could happen, and because of what? My sodding hat? A sweet street seller? A couple of gay guys?

A single word from a total stranger? Get with the program Olivier; you are so much smarter than that for god's sake. You REALLY let yourself down tonight big time and you let me down too.

I was so shocked and disappointed we barely spoke before midday the next day. He slept with his back to me in silence. I had nothing to say to him. He told me he was sorry before I left, that he was angry with himself but it was too late to take it back. Deeply unattractive trait; I never knew he was capable of jealous rages to that extent.

Major doubts had kicked in, in the Big Apple. I flew back that evening as planned, to be at the girls' Christmas carol concert that started at 11 a.m. the next morning. A hideous fat woman that smelt so badly of body odor actually put her hand down inside my knickers as she frisked me in Amsterdam airport en route back to London, which made me feel physically sick.

I was jet-lagged as well as spun out from the events of last night and my trip so much so I didn't get it at first, but as I flew from there to London I realized how far beyond the call of duty she had actually gone with me. OMG. I would have punched her in the face if I hadn't got so much going on in my mind at that moment. I begged the black cab driver to keep his foot flat to the floor whilst he enquired how my trip was. London cabbies are the best in the world for a grounding chat and a laugh with, even straight off the redeye from the States!

Thankfully I wasn't the last parent there as I fell in the doors trying to quickly straighten myself out at 11:03 a.m., hiding my weekend bag under my seat, only to seek out the girls' beaming smiles greeting me from the stage. Mummy's made it! Of course she has! I would never miss it for the world—I just had to travel three and a half thousand miles to be here, via a brief altercation with a filthy Dutch lesbian security officer. Nothing unusual there then, prior to her children's first carol concert in England!

"Hello everyone." If any of those 'stuck up their own ass' parents had seen what my last forty hours had consisted of, they probably would be staring at me even more intensely than they usually do, that's for sure. The performances were fantastic, reminding me that that was one of the events where the school fees actually went, thank god. Not on unqualified PE teachers teaching science but on things like this. Brilliant.

My girls shone like stars. Proud Mummy moment.

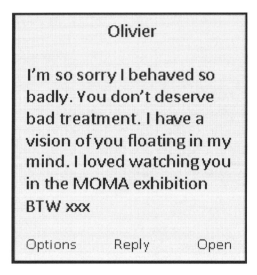

Olivier

I'm so sorry I behaved so badly. You don't deserve bad treatment. I have a vision of you floating in my mind. I loved watching you in the MOMA exhibition BTW xxx

Options Reply Open

Olivier

I can't stop thinking about you leaving for a long time over great distance. I wonder what the new year will bring us? I hate being apart from you, especially at this time of year. xxx

Options Reply Open

DECEMBER 20TH, 2005

I'm so bursting with chat! I can't wait to write this stuff down! I think I need to buy another book to write in soon. It's like an addiction. Once you start, when you are writing as you are thinking, it's so hard to stop. I think it's time I re-read this for the first time, to refresh my memory of the horrendous shit I've been dealing with, along with the monumental highs, of somehow still being in love.

Yes he is still married, so what. I think in my well-rehearsed line I've been defending myself to comments about seeing a married man who nearly eighteen months after we've been seeing each other, still hasn't left his wife! Too much to write, so I will do my best to read this book and write the rest in Thailand. That sounds like a bloody good idea. I've really missed writing.

Olivier	water on it. I know this
Morning darling. God I wish I could kiss you good morning everyday! We don't spend enough time together. It's like a wound that never heals, as it heals it's like someone puts salt	situation is unacceptable for you. I'm trying to find solutions. I love you, I love you, I love you! xxx
Options Reply Open	Options Reply Open

JANUARY 26TH, 2006

What was I thinking? Go to Thailand and write? You must be kidding. I can't work out whether it's just been that my roller coaster ride was going so fast that I couldn't breathe, or a tiredness that was so all consuming and overpowering that I couldn't even consider picking up this book to write. Now I'm back home, finally brushing my teeth and getting into bed, looking at my pj drawer (where I hide my diary) bursting with so much inside I just had to write something. I've been back in London five months.

I think I may be growing up. I'm using three creams on my face when I go to bed and sometimes I have drunk THREE glasses of wine by the time I lie looking at the ceiling, in hideous, nothing sexy about them, warm pajamas in total silence wondering how I got here. Great, isn't it? I hope where I'm going gets better. I'm hoping this stage is my 'waiting in transit' nights on the way to where I'm going. Not sure how much longer I can eat Weetabix with chopped up banana, with tons of sugar, in bed for my only comfort.

I NEED LOVING! I soooo do! Does that make me a weak person?

How have I found myself so reliant, on my weekends by myself with my children, on the odd text from a married man who lives in Geneva? It's sickening and pathetic.

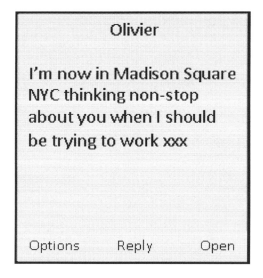

```
┌────────────────────────────────┐
│          Trouble               │
│                                │
│  Why don't you ever            │
│  respond? Are you abroad       │
│  again??                       │
│                                │
│                                │
│                                │
│                                │
│                                │
│  Options      Reply      Open  │
└────────────────────────────────┘
```

FEBRUARY 17TH, 2006

My first trip to Verbier, Switzerland, for Paul, a good friend of ten years plus, who asked me to help him redesign his bachelor pad. Good to go somewhere I've never been before and to be in the snow. Considering I always opt for the beach it's a novelty.

The first person I meet when we go out for dinner together happens to be the owner of a very famous hotel who is looking to redesign all the soft furnishings. I gave him my business card telling him I will do the job better than anyone else he's talking to. I really want the contract. I meet a whole new world of friends. I dance for the first time in years having reluctantly been dragged on the dance floor. I feel confident in myself. HOORAY!

Two weeks later I return to Verbier, where I meet an Italian playboy called Raphael for the first time, as two other friends and I are being booked by the police for illegally carrying three on a quad bike, down the mountain, after a four-hour lunch, during a whiteout. I'm on the front. Nice to meet you. After all this time waiting for Olivier I don't see the harm in remembering that he is not the only man on the planet. I should open my mind a little to other romances surely?

Two nights later, we are in the infamous Farm Club, as Raphael confidently starts to stroke the bottom of my leg whilst we are talking. OH NO! I have 'two-day stubble' so I say I have to shave them before he could ever do that again, half jokingly.

He said, "Fine, let's go." Go? Go where?

We leave the club and I find myself on the back of his quad bike, driving through the deep snow which is falling fast too, into the darkness, back to an electric gate opening to the lift, up to his incredible, vast chalet overlooking the mountaintops. This is hysterical!

I run a hot bath full of bubbles, shave my legs to the smoothness of a baby's bottom, get out, and get dressed to go and sit and talk by the fire whilst he strokes the bottom of my ankles for nearly two hours! Then I say "I've got to go, I'm leaving for the airport in an hour." I kiss him on the cheek goodbye, as he stands in his doorway watching me leave, with a look of complete bemusement that I have never seen before. "Goodnight."

I laughed the entire walk back to Paul's in the snow, just as the sun starts coming up. Ha! That was so fun and liberating …

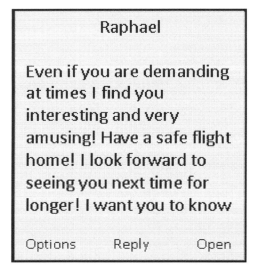

I need time to write this book. It drives me mad that I'm always so shattered that when I get any 'me time' I just quietly die and sleep. Or I go out because I get even more depressed if I don't get out and have a social life. I had dinner with Olivier in London a few days later which was rather strange, as the more I find myself and discover a new life here, the more he doesn't.

Olivier

I was trying to find a way to move forward without losing too much financially as I am committed to supporting my family. I explained it several times. If you love someone you

Options   Reply   Open

Don't look elsewhere. I saw you blushing when I asked you about Verbier. I was embarrassed for you. You will remember that your self esteem wasn't so low with me after a few inevitable stands. I was trying hard for you, for us,

Options   Reply   Open

I swear. Unless you have already found 'the one' in which case I take it all back. I was in love with you. I trusted you. I hope you will be ok because I've never felt for anyone what I feel for you. Good luck darling xxx

Options   Reply   Open

I'm at home now having dropped the girls with Tom. That was great. I was completely

ignored. He didn't even acknowledge me. He didn't even get out of the car. I didn't care

either. Jerk.

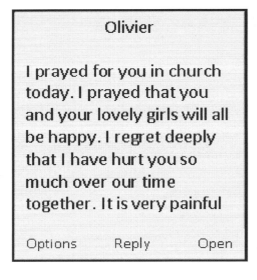

```
┌─────────────────────────────────┐
│          Raphael                │
│                                 │
│  I'm looking forward to         │
│  seeing you again. Next         │
│  time we won't be               │
│  strangers. Awesome             │
│  powder, wish you were          │
│  here to come up the            │
│  mountain with me xx            │
│                                 │
│  Options    Reply      Open     │
└─────────────────────────────────┘
```

Italian playboy?! Really?!

Olivier hasn't returned my texts for a week. I know it's over, but it's too hard to let go.

I want someone here to put moisturizer on my tan. I want someone to be in bed with me. Someone. I'm bored of sleeping alone. It's a weird learning curve to be alone so much. Why am I so bloody picky with my men?

I'm supposed to be exchanging contracts on a flat this weekend that I've found for me to convert. I'm knocking down three main walls, ripping out the kitchen and bathrooms to redesign it to an open plan, slick, cool pad, with lots of light and space. I've begged and borrowed from my parents to be able to get this, to do my magic on it, and sell it to pay school fees along with the rent for the next six months. The only problem is not having a bean to do the work.

Memo : Need to work on that tomorrow. Got to remember to eat too.

APRIL 24TH, 2006

"Take your chances while you can, you never know when they'll pass you by."

I'm getting slightly better at it all I think. I know more how I work, how I struggle, how I sink, and why I cry. Then something appears in the clearing ahead. I feel alive. I'm learning. I'm OK. I'm getting there. I feel stronger in waves, but each wave feels slightly closer to the shore. As they go up the beach they run all the way back down but when they come in again they crash a few inches further in. Just that glimpse of the completeness is so satisfying, that it gives me the overwhelming strength that somehow carries me through. I watch things unfold that I know are out of my control now. I've learned to sit back sometimes, to not waste my energy where I can't change the result.

I feel beautiful today. The first time in a long time, even though I haven't got anyone to tell me they think I am.

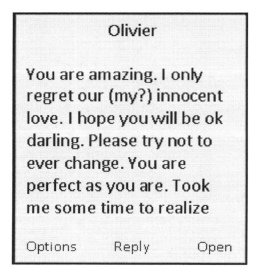

Olivier

You are amazing. I only regret our (my?) innocent love. I hope you will be ok darling. Please try not to ever change. You are perfect as you are. Took me some time to realize

Options   Reply   Open

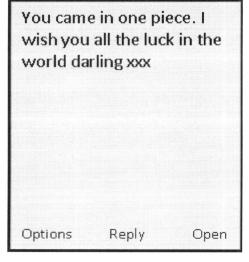

You came in one piece. I wish you all the luck in the world darling xxx

Options   Reply   Open

I missed Olivier today. I thought of him for hours. I miss the closeness. I miss his skin, his soft eyes and looking at the wonder in them when I talk about my life that he can't do. I wish he could. I wish I could do his life, but I can't do that one either.

Olivier

Most people open a packet
of biscuits when they want
to cheer themselves up. In
your case you book a
holiday to Barbados??!
xxx

Options   Reply   Open

Barbados. Spent money I don't have taking the girls to see their godmother Jules and Greg for ten days on their island. I think I want to buy a house in Ibiza. Maybe move there at the end of next year if I can earn enough money? I want to get my own career properly up and running once more as opposed to earning Tom money. The girls and I can do international again. We could base ourselves there. We can have the space, the health, the warmth, all the things I want the girls to have. Seeing them in Barbados reminded me of how happy they are outdoors all the time, not that I'd ever forgotten. In the water, on the beach and the only clothing being bikini bottoms.

We need a bigger garden. I need a bloody tumble dryer right now though! More than two foot of smoggy sun against a trellis in the back yard too would be great.

I've just realized that I'm single!! AND IT'S GREAT!!

APRIL 27TH, 2006

It's becoming more and more apparent that my luck seems to be changing. Thank god.

I have strong feelings more frequently that it just might be OK.

My god, what have I somehow accomplished inside after the last two years of going to hell and back again. I feel wiser and stronger than I've ever been before and I'm alone. Annoyingly my tan's fading with no man within reach to put Hawaiian Tropic on my body, but I seem to have just stumbled across the realization how capable I am rather than living in my husband's shadow, workwise. It feels wonderful. I'm being paid to do what I love the most. I've done it ALL BY MYSELF!

I won a hotel contract in Verbier. I bought and I'm developing a lovely flat on the common in London. I've managed to provide my first three terms of school fees for my babies. I can make it. I can make it. I can make it.

```
┌─────────────────────────────┐
│          Olivier            │
│                             │
│  I wish that all the dark   │
│  clouds over us would one   │
│  day let a ray of sunshine  │
│  through xxx                │
│                             │
│                             │
│                             │
│  Options    Reply    Open   │
└─────────────────────────────┘
```

Olivier is in NYC, in a taxi, calling telling me he can't live without me.

Raphael is at some amazing glamorous party in St Tropez probably sleeping with drop-dead supermodels that are dying to have his children and live between his eighteen properties across the world. Good luck to them.

None of which is any help for the Hawaiian Tropic dilemma.

I made myself a wonderful filet steak, with scrummy garlic butter, and looked up my website that I'm working on, which made me feel good. Hate our mouse house though, got to get out of here. New phone. New life! 248 numbers in my phone now.

Everything just might be falling into place. I think I can even pay the school fees again.

This 'gravy on this dish' sure tastes pretty damn good. If I'm really lucky I might even sleep tonight too.

Olivier

I have been observing you over the past three months drifting away from me when I was trying hard (obviously not hard enough) and now I'm totally destroyed. All the

Options   Reply   Open

confidence I've built through knowing you and the pride I had to be with you is gone. I loved your madness and the way you gave yourself. You don't owe me any explanation

Options   Reply   Open

APRIL 29TH, 2006

I've reached the cutoff point with Olivier. He's coming on Monday to take me out for dinner, yet I feel like I've closed the book on a future together, so what's the point? I'm also over being taken out for $400 dinners only to come home and have to pay $75 for my babysitters. I just can't afford it nor do I want to. I'd rather eat in and, cook a delicious dinner with a lovely bottle of wine for a fraction of the cost. (He never offers to pay the sitters and it's not his responsibility either, but it still bugs me). Of course I'd like to see him, but I know it wouldn't be a happy evening for either of us; far from it. It was all I ever wanted, but I don't think I want it now. It's too late, and for the right reasons.

MAY 2ND, 2006

Oh, how easy life would have been if I could have survived on the crumbs Tom gave me emotionally and spiritually. If only I could have sacrificed wholeness, in order to simply be 'comfortable'.

I miss my house so much.

I miss my dogs, like missing a limb.

I miss my garden.

I miss the sunshine.

I actually miss Tom too. Working with him, and all our team of boys that I loved so much. All the laughter between us all on site. All the projects we created together. As a team nobody could compete with Tom and me. We were unstoppable in what we could achieve. When will these clouds all disappear?

I pulled the weeds from my two-foot square flowerbed today, looking at a fifteen-foot high brick wall.

June 11th, 2006

I just laughed at myself when I heard myself asking "Who can I ring that can tell me everything's going to be OK?" How ridiculous is that? I can only call myself.

"Hi, is that you?'

"Yes."

"Well I hope I'm not disturbing you but I needed to tell you something. Just for the record, everything is going to be just fine, I assure you."

"Really? Are you serious? How do you know for sure?"

"Just trust me. I know."

"Oh that's so great to hear, thank you so much."

"No problem, I'm always here for you. I am actually you, so we do genuinely have a direct line if you ever need me, I'm here twenty four seven for you …"

Daisy went under general anesthetic today for a little operation she needed. I woke up at 6 a.m. covered in sweat, probably having nightmares about it, either that or in sympathy for my baby. She was under by 9 a.m. I watched her eyes rolling into the back of her head, as she laughed with the doctors, oblivious to Mummy struggling like mad.

I think one of the most flooring emotions is watching your child disappearing into another world, out of your control, in the hands of strangers. I was carefully guided out of the theatre to wait anxiously alone outside. Everything went well. Mission accomplished. I'm absolutely shattered by the whole experience though.

Olivier	
I know Daisy went to hospital today and I'm hoping it all went well. I've been thinking about how tough this all must be for you, doing all that you do for them alone. All the	Stress and worry for you and I can't help much either. I can guess where she gets her bravery! xxx
Options Reply Open	Options Reply Open

Tom's being slightly reasonable, for the first time in months. Miracles will never cease. He must have a new girlfriend. Olivier's so wonderful still, even though he isn't my future. All Raphael's missed calls. I haven't responded; I'm absolutely dead.

Exchanging contracts finally on the flat in the morning.

Late paying school fees.

Moving next month into our new home, a converted little chapel.

Am I ever going to calm down and make some time? Will I ever let it happen? Will I ever be able to afford to just chill out? I'm dead, two weeks after Barbados and it feels like I never went. Even losing my tan faster than usual! Bollocks.

Got a date tomorrow with a really fun character from Verbier, with his chauffeur picking me up at 7.30 pm. I have a streaming cold. Great. Sleep, sleep, sleep required.

Trouble

I am coming over now to see if you are still awake. Answer your phone please?

Options   Reply   Open

MAY 13TH, 2006

My first Saturday in London, without being away for my weekend off, I spent sleeping all morning. I'm so run down; I am not looking after myself. Raphael, Olivier, Trouble, Maxine (a random surgeon I met at a drinks party), who else is offering to take me out this evening? Tonight my choice is not to be out with anyone, to be here alone in my bed, to relax, to chill the hell out with lots of food, no booze, followed by a full night's sleep.

Olivier

We are like fire and water or diamond and glass if you prefer which is why we are so attracted to each other. You always want definitive answers. You go straight to the last page of the book

Options   Reply   Open

when I like to read it. I could handle you if you weren't permanently in the market for someone better than me when we both know he doesn't exist xxx

Options   Reply   Open

MAY 15TH, 2006

Feel back to normal, whatever normal is, healthwise anyway. Tried to keep sleeping when I woke up but my mind wouldn't let me go back for long. Too much to think about, can't believe it's two pages from the end of this first fat book.

I've come so far yet I've still got so far to go. I feel sometimes like I'm propelling myself and holding my breath at the same time. Maybe the more risks I take, the more I'm taking. I may die tomorrow so what the hell.

I think my biggest problem is lack of faith in myself. It's only me that holds me back. Sometimes I find I feel so scared of thinking big now. I never used to. I think I'm scared because of the girls. I'm afraid of screwing it all up for them. I want to give them all I possibly can. I don't want to let them down. I want to be able to pay their school fees as well as buy them the roller skates that I've been promising them for ages. I want to be in the park with them and get to that place I want to be with them, even though we aren't in the country.

```
┌─────────────────────────────┐
│        Trouble              │
│                             │
│ Poo why won't you let me    │
│ come and see you?           │
│                             │
│                             │
│                             │
│                             │
│                             │
│                             │
│                             │
│ Options    Reply     Open   │
└─────────────────────────────┘
```

How much do I fight with myself about the country? I don't want to be in the country, not the country here in the UK! I would die of boredom. I would go absolutely mad.

I'm not part of it anymore, and even when I was, I didn't want to be there with only the locals for inspiration. I want to be on the pulse of life, not wishing I was; not stuck in a muddy lane with one sad local pub, where except at the weekends you only ever see people with blue rinses and thick glasses who dribble when they eat.

MAY 22ND, 2006

Everytime I think, right, that's it, put a line underneath what I've written, call it a day and re-read your life for the past two years, something else mad happens and I just have to write about it or I will burst. Considering the last week's entertainment, it would be sad to omit this sequence of events.

OK, last Tuesday I was rushing around all day in order to leave London in to drive two hours down to my parents' business in Wiltshire. They had sold up and it was handover evening, so I floored it there with a bottle of champagne to surprise them, quick toast, then drove back all the way to London by 9 pm.

I went straight to Harrods for a drinks party where I had agreed to meet a surgeon I'd met at a drinks party last week. The whole affair looked hideous, full of stiffs, so I didn't even go in. Bullshitted to him that I wasn't back in London yet and headed straight to Zuma to meet Fi and had a scream. Surgeon rang me all evening, I didn't answer. Hate that desperation; it's the ultimate turnoff. So unappealing and needy. Yuck.

```
┌─────────────────────────────┐
│          Surgeon            │
│                             │
│  Hi yummy mummy. I'm not    │
│  feeling too much like the  │
│  good doctor today so I'm   │
│  taking it easy listening to│
│  jazz CD's! What about      │
│  dinner sometime? x         │
│                             │
│                             │
│  Options    Reply    Open   │
└─────────────────────────────┘
```

```
┌─────────────────────────────┐
│          Trouble            │
│                             │
│  What do you mean I'm       │
│  disturbing you? You have   │
│  disturbed me from the      │
│  moment I met you. I'm      │
│  coming over now.           │
│                             │
│                             │
│                             │
│  Options    Reply    Open   │
└─────────────────────────────┘
```

Wednesday—Trouble turns up unannounced the minute the girls are in bed.

Thursday—Raphael is due in town for dinner. He misses his flight. It's raining and 13 degrees in London, so he asks if he can fly me to Milan instead. No thanks.

Trouble takes me for dinner at the Blue Bird on the King's Road and I think for the first time, he's actually good fun and quite attractive.

Friday—I get up and head down to Sussex with the girls for the weekend at Kristy and Ralph's house, which is like our second home. We all have a long walk in the country before a call comes in from Fi telling me to get my ass back up to town for a night on the tiles. "Really? I'm too tired."

"No you have to; you will never believe who you are hanging out with later."

Have I got the strength? I snuggle the girls in and drive back up to town, kick off my walking boots, wrap on a pair of heels and jeans, run a brush through my hair, filling my tired eyes in the cab with the infamous eye dew en route to Chelsea.

I walk in to champagne cocktails, slippery nipples and a very handsome young Royal who's sitting down next to me. We discovered mutual friends we had in Oz that we had been kangaroo shooting with, which was very entertaining for us both. After shared stories of the outback, we laughed, we danced, and we had a hilarious evening.

Masses of security, lots of sugary lollies, ice cube fights, fluoro spray, bacon sandwiches at dawn, and more fun than I can remember having in a very long time.

He literally shocked the hell out of me, taking my breath away when he lifted me off the floor against the wall and kissed me at the end of the night. Now that was a world-class kiss!! I was numb from it and took me a few seconds to regroup before I accepted another one, which was even sweeter than the first!

I rolled into bed at 5 a.m. having been dropped home by him and the fleet of Ranges. He even got out and walked me to my front door before planting a final kiss on my cheek goodnight. I'm sure if any of my neighbors had looked out of their window they would not believe who was outside!!

Thanks for an incredible night!

Hmmmmm.

Waking up to think to yourself 'Did last night really happen?' isn't something I'm used, to, as I have a memory like an elephant. Ha! Dropped home by the hottest Royal, huh?

 I had such a brilliant evening with him.

Oh, to be a 21-year-old princess! What a character. I looked at my phone at his texts to me after he had dropped me off. What a honey. What a laugh. What a lucky girl I am!

I drove straight back down to Ralph and Kristy's in time for one of their immaculate Sunday lunches. The girls had only just got up, still in their pj's, and were jumping on the trampoline having a ball with their best friend Scarlett, Ralph and Kristy's lovely daughter. As I kissed Ralph hello, I eyed up the tray of roast potatoes over his shoulder, counting them like I always do. Were there 18 for me today? I'm starving!

"So those lips of yours last kissed a Royal goodnight then, did they?" He teased. We all laughed as I relayed the hilarious night. I was shattered. I spent the rest of the weekend mucking around with all the kids before the trip back to town homework done, ready for a new week.

Trouble

Never had an affair before so FYI you are not one of many!

Options   Reply   Open

Olivier

Thanks to you I have lived
the most exciting moments
of my life. I know that
because I know that
because I spent all last
night going back through
every one of them starting

Options   Reply   Open

two years ago when I first
saw you in that restaurant.
I saw the light of the sun
when you walked in. Since
then i have thought about
you a million times I
promise I will never forget
any of it. You are such a
wonderful and unique

Options   Reply   Open

person. You will always
have lots of people who
love you... I'm ruined xxx

Options   Reply   Open

June 23rd, 2006

I'm spending my days on another dusty site in the flat I've bought, overseeing smashing down walls and designing the space. It's great to be so busy though, doing what I do best. It's just around the corner from the school so it's perfect. Wonder if we should move in rather than sell it?

When I woke up last Monday morning it was before my alarm went off, aware of a commotion outside. Lots of talking, cars and people. Bleary eyed, I got up to look out of the bathroom window. It took several seconds to work out what was going on.

My entire street was full of press centered around OUR front door. Oh my god! Oh my god.

I froze, two seconds later, as the girls came downstairs wondering what was happening outside. Now that was an interesting conversation. Thankfully I'm very straight up with my girls. They knew all about my evening's entertainment with the Royal a few weeks ago and after a couple of minutes digesting what was happening they both thought it was a hugely entertaining way to start the week. I didn't. I just pretended I was absolutely fine, that I was just going to have a five minute FREAK OUT!!

After phoning two or three girlfriends on advice as to what to do next, I decided to do nothing. I'd ask Ju, my best friend from school, if she could come over on her way and collect the girls. I would just sit tight. There was NO WAY I was going out that door.

They would have to go away eventually. I sat listening to my landline, my mobile as well as my front door bell ringing all day and night. Answer phone full. How did they get all my numbers? Reminded me of the days when Tom would ring 1400 times a day.

SHIT!! SHIT!! SHIT!! What could I do to get rid of them? If you stand with your ear to the front of a terraced house in London you can pretty much hear everything, so I sat in my kitchen on my phone with the doors shut, completely spun out as to what to do. They didn't leave. In fact they grew in numbers, as it seemed the longer I said nothing, the more the speculations were growing. Someone must have been stirring the pot.

Who would have done that?

That night a reporter was calling out my name through the letterbox. I pretended to be the foreign au pair who couldn't speak English, who had no idea where I was. I wasn't there though. Amber laughed so much she couldn't breathe, hiding with Daisy at the top of the stairs. That was the only funny part of the dilemma we were in!

"42-year-old mother of two seduces 21-year-old Royal" was the headline read to me by Ju over the phone, the following day, out of a well-read trashy paper. REALLY? This was almost laughable. Especially the 42-year-old bit? Adding 9 years to my age surely would provoke me to say something? Bastards! It went from being something I thought would just fizzle out eventually and grew into this overnight. We couldn't stay at the house anymore.

It was too much living solely in the kitchen as it was the only safe place out of earshot or eyes looking down our hallway. Day after day they refused to leave.

Tom rang me saying there were two reporters chasing him up the harbor in Menorca trying to dig dirt from my 'estranged husband,' and asking me what the hell had I done now? Now that was a funny conversation—not. He said he was getting off the island and that the school the girls used to attend had reporters prowling there too; even where I used to have my morning coffee after the school run.

Two or three press had been on the gates of the school here in London for over two weeks without a break, trying desperately to see if I would take the girls so they could get their 'Mummy' shot. Naturally I had to inform the school what was going on, again, another delightful conversation. The headmistress told me how sorry she was for me and how awful it must be, whilst she almost rubbed her hands in glee with the publicity of the rumors of the girls being smuggled in and out of classes. A Royal connection for her to boast about now. Everyone was talking about us. It was seriously embarrassing.

Our 87-year-old neighbor in Sussex, from years ago, had been offered thousands in return for information on my whereabouts. Reporters in all the restaurants and bars I used to go to. This could not be real, surely? I did nearly three weeks of barely eating, hardly sleeping in random friend's houses with the girls, stressing beyond belief before I picked up my phone to ring a reporter who had been ringing me consistently since the start.

"Just how big is your bosses' budget to follow me and my family around over Europe? When are you going to quit it?" He couldn't believe it was me that was calling him.

"My boss says when it comes to you, Catherine, there is no budget. We won't stop until we get something; it's too big for us to not have a bite of. If there's nothing going on, why don't you just say that? Say something rather than nothing. Put the record straight and then we will leave you in peace I promise." I told him I would think about it.

I talked to my lawyers, my parents, and my good friends. The pressure on my girls, my family, the school, my friends, my ex-husband hiding in Spain, anyone associated with me was way too much. It all made me sick. It was the last thing I or anyone else needed, for god's sake. Payback for one of the funniest nights of my life?

My plan was that they would get bored and leave me alone. It hadn't worked. I gave one interview, on the understanding that it would be three quarters of a page max, so I made up a load of crap to feed them. I had done nothing wrong, so I shouldn't have to suffer this bollocks anymore, nor should anyone else I knew. Tell them something, be done with it. It would be published on Sunday.

I found it hard to trust anyone at all as to my whereabouts. Katie came to London to see an exhibition, so I asked her whilst she was here if she would mind doing me a big favor going to my house to get us all some clean clothes etc. I warned her not to talk to anyone outside, that they would be bound to provoke her to say something. I spoke to the black cabbie telling him that I would give him details where he was taking her, only once she came out of the house. I knew that the paparazzi would have been on to him whilst she was inside, which of course they were.

Fat lenses pushed in her face as she rushed in and out along with the questions. When she was safely back in the car with a bag of clothes and underwear (she said that she couldn't work out which were bras and which were knickers, they were all so small!) I spoke to the driver again and told him where I was. He then drove her out to the train station where cars can't stop, so the pursuing press had no option but to drive by. At which point he told her to get down so they couldn't see her as they spun around the roundabout and back to see an empty cab, leading them to think she had got a train. They disappeared. Then he drove

her to meet me, three blocks away, where I opened the door to see a red-faced, stressed-out

Katie sitting back up in her seat! Top driver. Top man. Top tip. What a joke this all was!

She left with mild anxiety, back to my father's, and I felt awful she had had a piece of my

life today. Sorry Katie!

Trouble called just as I was running down the King's Road trying to escape a photographer,

and I hung up on him.

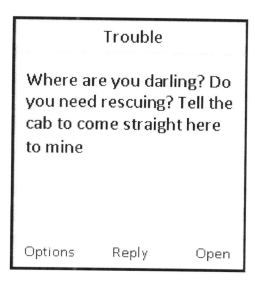

Trouble

Where are you darling? Do you need rescuing? Tell the cab to come straight here to mine

Options   Reply   Open

I called Trouble back.

I did want rescuing and agreed to see Trouble. When we sat in his kitchen making me laugh, as he always did, I felt like he had waited so long and I actually was ready to surrender to him. He had definitely worn my barriers down over all these months of relentless pursuit.

The girls went to stay for the weekend with my parents whilst I left to hide away at

Raphael's rooftop penthouse in Milan. When I arrived there he was entertaining two stunning women and another guy who all thought it was a great idea to drive two hours to a party until dawn at some incredible location. I couldn't think of anything I'd rather do less so I climbed into his bed, bid them all farewell and slept for nearly twenty-four hours straight, alone. I got up, with not much to say to the 'playboy extraordinaire' who had fallen back through the door only an hour ago, and left to fly on to my friend Thoes' villa in a remote village outside St Tropez until the storm had passed. I was so relieved to see him and be safe there with him, I probably hugged him to within an inch of his life.

"Today's newspapers are tomorrow's fish and chip wrappers, don't worry about it!" Viv laughed, reassuring me on the phone. I kept trying to remember that. I hadn't spoken to her for ages so it was good to hear her sympathetic, understanding voice. Nothing ever fazed her.

We sat there in the warmth on Thoes' terrace at midnight whilst he looked up online the article that would be all over the papers in the morning. When I read it I felt sick.

I had my first brush with what the press are capable of and how they twist anything you say. Jesus. It was also nearly THREE pages of exaggerated rubbish.

I couldn't sleep for hours petrified of what the repercussions would be now, having read that.

My first text, of dozens of the day, woke me up at 8 am from my mother.

How could you? Thanks for that message Mum. Good question though. I could ask you the same question tenfold. She had absolutely no idea what the girls and I had been through for the past month. All she ever cared about was what her neighbors would think.

As always, in her eyes, I had brought it all upon myself.

I flew home, picked the girls up and when we got back to London the press had given up camping on our doorstep. Mission accomplished. We carried on our lives, a little wiser than before. I could take the girls to and from school again, and walk around freely in our mouse house.

I met up with the Royal a few weeks later, whereupon he put his arm around me apologizing for what I'd been subjected to. He knew everything, right down to the dramas at the school gates. I said sorry too for having to say something. He understood and we both laughed about some of the lines in the article! I teased him that the pictures of him and me, sitting in an empty bath fully dressed that night would be on auction soon! Only he and I knew, and only he and I will ever know, what really went on that wild evening. That's the way it was always going to stay. Opinions are like assholes; everybody has one.

```
┌─────────────────────────────────┐
│           Trouble              ⸙ │
│                                  │
│  You are the most beautiful      │
│  girl on the planet in Ugg       │
│  boots... I would love to        │
│  spend the entire day            │
│  making loved to you.            │
│                                  │
│                                  │
│                                  │
│  Options      Reply       Open   │
└─────────────────────────────────┘
```

When I read that I thought, you know what? That sounds like a really good idea. He was definitely beginning to win me over. Shit!

What about our new home? Why have I felt like I can't do it again? Self doubt? I will get back what I put in. I have now, after seven months back in London, bought a flat to transform into someone's dream home and sell. Maybe that's an achievement, but I can do it walking on my hands, so it hasn't really fulfilled me much.

Why do I doubt myself, when it's only a flat, for god's sake? Am I afraid of how capable I am? Of course I can do it, and make money. I have absolutely no security. I'm on the edge right now. The past three or four weeks I haven't been able to get to sleep. Racing mind. My only worry is supporting the girls and I couldn't care less about anything else. That's all I do. I hate Tom for paying so little towards his girls; I can't believe he's leaving it all up to me.

Lines around my eyes and a wrinkly stomach as I'm so skinny doesn't mean the end for me! I can't believe I've got all these men wanting to take me out. I'M SINGLE! For the first time in my life, officially single. Since the age of 16, I only had three long-term relationships going straight from one to the other so being free to do ANYTHING I like is GREAT!

Olivier lost it badly with me for the third time. Three strikes and you're out. He went absolutely mad with jealousy about me having dinner with another guy, who I had met through a friend; regarding doing deals together, nothing more. I've lived with him having dinners with his wife all this time and he protests about me trying to get on in my work? Mad. He shouted at me, sealing something I didn't want to acknowledge—it was the end. Another end….

It's OK though. Now he has left his wife, like he was always destined to, he's starting on a scary, self-discovery journey of his own to find happiness. My father was right (again)! Olivier really was my angel sent to guide me through the worst time in my life. He gave me the confidence to change my life. I know that now. I forgive him for all the hurt and I hope he can forgive me too one day. I know more than anyone what he's living through day after day right now. We were never going to end up together. Our worlds were too far apart.

```
┌─────────────────────────────────┐
│                                 │
│            Trouble              │
│                                 │
│   I'm dying to see you. Been    │
│   talking about you all night   │
│   to Mick. Could it work or     │
│   are you too mad? In the       │
│   mean time can I secretly      │
│   make love to you?             │
│                                 │
│                                 │
│  Options      Reply      Open   │
│                                 │
└─────────────────────────────────┘
```

I still don't know who can handle me, but I definitely know that Olivier couldn't.

He wanted to, he believed he could but a tiny part of me thinks I always knew in the back of my mind he couldn't. I had to believe in something back then. I can't sacrifice who I am for him or anyone ever again.

Here it is, the last page of my thick, stripy book! That's really going to force me to go to the stationary shop to carry on my ranting later today…

Hope? Abundance of it.

Faith? A fair bit.

Trust? Not too much.

Confidence? Days of feeling capable of conquering the word, alongside days of still wanting to die.

Love? Don't ask. Going to work harder on that.

Truth? More, and more and more if it. However much it can hurt me, I prefer it!

I wish I stopped holding myself back as I'm on the edge of the next cliff, when I've jumped so many and I'm somehow still alive!

This new book was so blank; I didn't even know which way to start writing in it. Back or front? Which way around? That must say it all!

"If I lay here, if I just lay here, would you lie with me and just forget the world? All that I am, all that I ever was, is here in your perfect eyes there all I can see. I need your grace to remind me to find my own..."

Snow Patrol plays. I dream about Trouble who after nearly a year of plaguing me, I have at last let into my life and he has already hurt me. I must have been like a game to him. Moving house a week today...

All normal, secure and confident?

None of the above. All totally unusual. Completely insecure and lacking in any confidence whatsoever – good. Good to be honest with myself!

What time is my flight tomorrow to Verbier? I'm sure it is after lunch. I could sleep for a week.

I spend an hour and forty-five minutes on the phone to Katie tonight. I had the longest email from Olivier at midnight, plus I've had Tom on the phone wanting to go away for a few days—he is currently drunk and out of control at some fiesta in Menorca. If he really wanted me, for me, he would be on my doorstep tonight. Those are the sad true facts. He never did, he didn't, and he still doesn't. Why does he do this to me??

I DONT WANT HIM EITHER! How much clearer do I need to see the way it is?

How much more writing on the wall do I need to see? I know I am stupid, but surely I can't be *that* stupid?

I've just written down all Trouble's texts, which was really therapeutic—all the messages on my phone from a beautiful, random man, whom I never took any attention of—who after ten months has got into me and into my bed. Lovely, lovely, lovely but so used me and I let him. It's OK, another lesson learnt—Great lover, great fun but a dead-end future.

OK, so here I am on the way to Verbier again. Must be my 9th or 10th trip here to plan this hotel project—it's a long old road. Up at 5:45 a.m. I've only been here twice before with Raphael. He's in Ibiza. Couldn't sleep at all last night thinking about my book, my life, moving house, my lack of enough income, unsold flat, school fees and my empty bed. The nights are so long as I turn left, right, and then left and right again—is that because I can, because I have the space and freedom?

Katie said to me last night, "Grab hold of the things that you love, and let go of the things that you don't." I know she meant Tom and she is right. I still have yet to reach the realization of why he has an incredible power over me. I have to keep eating....

As I got up this morning I was reminded that summer is almost gone and the darkest mornings will be upon me soon, my least-favorite time of year. I find it so hard embracing the day in the dark and the cold, dragging myself out of bed like an ancient woman- I think I need to make more plans like a class or two—more yoga? More cooking lessons? I will be eternally grateful for my live-in chef who taught me how to cook really well.

I am looking forward to that. It's been a very long time since I have been able to entertain at home, and I think I'm going to have a Christmas party too.

Having those messages from Olivier made me so upset the other night it made me physically sick too. Those, along with Tom asking me to go away with him for a few days—how could this be all happening?

I had a lovely email from Olivier basically blaming me for ruining us—for not waiting for him and making me feel so bad for the fact that he is alone—he left his wife and children and then I am not there—is it all my fault? I don't think so in reality—it's not fair. Maybe he finds it easier to blame me rather than him. It happened, we aren't together and we never will be. There are reasons and I know that it must be destiny. He will find somebody else—some quiet and beautiful, intelligent woman.

Tom needed his 'mumsy' type and Olivier needed his 'opera lover.' I know that he will end up happy and so will I—I've just got to get my head stuck into work and stop worrying. Keep going, keep going, and keep going!

What makes me happy? My girls, my dogs, my work, my garden, my music, sunshine, outdoors......

I'm sitting alone in a bar in Verbier, having had dinner alone, so great though. I spent five hours measuring up my hotel: 94 pairs of curtains, 53 bedspreads. I'm designing these stunning cushions to put on the beds with the crown logo. It's going to look great.

September 9th, 2006

Last day of summer holidays with the girls. Longleat Safari Park, flat battery. Last car in the car park. Got home at 10:30 p.m.—five hours later. We made it, it is fine. Sometimes I surprise myself, and sometimes I think, "Fool, you know it doesn't have to be so hard." Paid school fees for this term, paid the deposit on the new house, paid car insurance again, bought bunk beds etc. etc. Great! Got my serious hotel project that I can't find enough hours in the day for but has to be finished in two weeks.

Olivier has been in touch wanting to take me for dinner when he is back from Singapore at the end of the month. Don't know how I feel there. Want to see him but don't know how it will be and how I will feel—I just don't know.

I know one thing though—I HATE MY SODDING EX-HUSBAND!!! He made a huge gesture of buying the girls the biggest, heaviest, space-taking TV, but wouldn't pay for delivery so I would have to drive miles out of London to get it. And it is too big to get in the car with the girls with me so I have decided to leave it there. Sod it. He can get it here. Tosser.

Things to do tomorrow:

Extend overdraft

Hang pictures

Put together bunk beds

Get stuff into storage

Choose colors for the hotel

Lose it with the AA for not being the fourth emergency service

Eat

Keep going

Don't panic

September 12th, 2006

My last night at Talbon St, Southwest London. I'm sure my neighbors will miss me and all the drama and entertainment that having me and the girls living here has brought over the past few months, or maybe they won't. At least the press may not find me for a while now.

Boxes everywhere—again! Chaos. Shit everywhere and to top it all I WAS BINNED TODAY by Trouble! Nice timing. Why not come over, grab a coffee on the way, and help me move house, put together a couple of beds, hang some mirrors, grab a take away and then bin me? No. He decided to bin me at the beginning of the day. Cheers then.

Why the hell I am still bothering to let myself get messed around by such an idiot is beyond me. All my friends think he's a total jerk. Treats me like a doormat and I still go back every time he calls.

What is it about this man, who happens to be a mere boy in every way? Can't think about it right now, too busy. The best thing about today was the fact I didn't have a ticket or a clamp when I went to retrieve my car with my throbbing head from the King's Road this morning. That was great, a real bonus..... $180 not going to line the pockets of Chelsea and Westminster council today.

At the bottom of one of my wardrobes I came across the box of all the things I kept from my time with Olivier. Why I kept them I never really understood myself. For me maybe because it had been so magical that I had to have something to keep, to touch, and to prove it was real. From boarding passes, to opera tickets, to love letters and pictures. That period of my life was definitely real. He once said at the beginning we could be passing planets, yet our paths crossed for a long time in the universe. I didn't want to look inside. I was too tired, too sad and not strong enough to think. I don't want to remind myself of something else, someone else that I've given up, who is now gone. All the lovely parts of being with somebody special. I do miss him. A lot. I miss talking to him. I miss looking at him. I miss cuddling him and I miss holding hands.

I so don't miss the 7 a.m. taxis annoyingly beeping their horns. I don't miss the feeling of rolling back in the duvet, having watched the man I love leaving, immaculately dressed in his Savile Row suit, smelling like a god, returning to his other life. I don't miss his phone being off at weekends or the tearful goodbyes at airports.

He has gone and he will never come back. He wasn't the one. But he was the one to start me on my journey of renewed self-awareness and self-worth. And he showed me how to feel, to be aware of all kinds of love again, however briefly.

So tomorrow, new house, get excited. Another rented waste of money. I can't, wish I could, but in my heart all I want is to be by the sea with the girls and the dogs in the sunshine. Not stuck in traffic for twenty minutes to get three blocks in the miserable rain.

Instead of that enormous beautiful palm tree, pool and gardens, I've been looking out onto a ten square foot piece of concrete with one single rose struggling to get up to see some light. Autumn is drawing closer and I'm here again, by myself, freaking out about money and how the hell I'm supposed to pay for everything for the girls and I without any help? I never signed up for this, did I?

But I remind myself I made my bed, and my god I would rather be in it alone than next to someone I didn't want to wake up with. I'm so lonely inside it's ridiculous. I miss being cuddled and curled up by the fire.

After everything I have been through and done to get here, after all I have given up and those mountains I've climbed, I'm still desperately lost and don't seem to be able to find any direction... I'm finding it SO hard to keep positive for the girls and me when I feel like I'm on a treadmill daily, almost paralyzed with fear of being able to sustain a stable life for us, when I'm under such pressure paying for them and I'm alone.

Things to do tomorrow: Move house (again), increase overdraft, and remember to eat.

Not drink a whole bottle of wine to myself or smoke a whole pack of Marlboro Lights.

Not think about the idiot that has binned me for the fifth time. Get my head into work and remind myself:

I CAN DO THIS

I CAN DO THIS

I CAN DO THIS

In the meantime, my shoulders feel like rocks. I'm so stressed out. I'm too tired to even make something to eat and the fridge is bare again. Bottle of 85 Margaux and some fish and chips sounds like the best option tonight. I still have my standards! Considering I don't drink red wine anymore it was sensational. One of 40 left by mistake from the previous owner of the house!! Not often you have a dinner party, run out of booze after some late arrivals, look in the shed and discover a vintage wine collection. I had them valued and could have sold them for thousands.

Let's not kid ourselves—I really needed every penny, but preferred to give them away to grateful friends. My father enjoyed a few, including a 1971 bottle from the year of my birth.

The landlord was a real scrooge. A selfish, mean, pathetic excuse of a man who did nothing to assist us when the electrics crashed, when we had no heating or hot water for days; or when the oven blew up; he didn't even bother to return my calls. He just charged me astronomical rent every month. So I didn't feel too guilty. Not after the second bottle was opened that night anyway!

I feel so old tonight. Any looks I have are fading faster than I can keep up with. I can now vouch for the fact that all those expensive creams that defy the years (or the effects of acrimonious divorce) are a complete bullshit waste of money.

"Oh Amber, I feel so old now," I said whilst we looked in the mirror together brushing our teeth one night.

"Mummy, you aren't getting older, you hardly ever get older," she smiled up at me, nuzzling her head into me affectionately. Another priceless Amber statement!

Does anyone feel like I do? I find it hard to believe that I'm the only one. Being a single parent is such incredible, relentless hard work. The ultimate responsibility. I never know if I'm doing the right thing, whether my girls will hate me for being me when they grow up. Sometimes I think I was meant to have my babies to keep me here, because they do. If I had ever turned that wheel to the right driving at a hundred miles an hour in the fast lane, then that would have devastated their lives along with hurting so many others.

I can still see my father's face when Tom had walked into my father's kitchen having driven off with my handbag with my phone. Even though we were separated, we had both gone to collect the girls from my parents, the day the penny dropped with him having watched me send a text to Olivier.

I had been for a long walk with my father sharing my sadness with him only a few weeks before, when he asked me outright if there was someone else. I had lied to him. Something I wasn't proud of. I never told him untruths. He was way to worldly wise to not be able to handle anything his youngest daughter threw his way. I wanted so badly to tell him. The only reason I hadn't, was because I knew he would think, like the rest of the world, that this was the only reason I wanted out. It never was the reason but I didn't think anyone would believe me.

I remember the look in his eyes, the sadness in his face as he plunged his hands into his pockets in silence, taking a deep breath as he heard those sickening words from Tom's mouth. The reason for that ultimate pain was his knowing I hadn't been honest with him, that I'd lied to him.

Where the hell is my knight in shining armor when I need him? To cook a beautiful dinner for me, run me a bath, give me a full massage and then make love to me?

Ah, yes...that's right, get real, he doesn't exist and that is the end of tonight's tale!

Tomorrow is another day though. He might be on his way?

I lost my temper with the girls tonight. A result of my stress when my patience ran out, and now I'm really angry with myself. It's not their fault that I'm suffering like mad with the pressure.

My hotel job I've barely been able to make any progress on—I'm going to only have eight weeks to do EVERYTHING! No computer connection still. Twat of a landlord, who is reneging on all he said he would do for me now I've moved in and he's got me. Hate renting. I'm not a teenager anymore.

Need to sell the flat, which still hasn't sold.

Need to look after myself.

Need a man and a van to come and move all my boxes into storage and hang pictures for me on Sunday.

Need to get the house in order.

Need to get laid. (But not by Trouble.)

Need some time out to get on with my work so badly. Tom is getting the girls tomorrow. Need a break. Poisoned myself with white wine on Tuesday and spent the day trying to work whilst being sick. When will I ever grow up?

Need a massage.

Still upset over Trouble, haven't spoken to him for ten days now. Very tired so I'm in bed by 9:30. God I never knew I would still get feelings of such emptiness in my stomach. So lonely....

Trouble

Fancy a nice glass of wine and some pretzels darling?

Options   Reply   Open

SEPTEMBER 18TH, 2006

Now I'm sitting at Geneva airport having just had a run in with Tom on the phone. He told me that his parents were doing me a big favor having the girls? He was eight days late bringing them home to me? This week was always his week and conveniently he forgot.

I made my meetings in Verbier, organized the moving date and everything because it was ALWAYS his week—asshole! So now I have to fly back, drive all the way to his parents and then drive ALL the way back to London; GREAT. AND have the girls when I'm moving house. I don't want them to experience even more upheaval.

Eight hours of unnecessary traveling on top of my week. He is the most manipulative person on the planet. I can't wait to be divorced!

Please God, if there is one, and you are listening—please help me cope better with this man who twists my brain, causes me such grief and upset, who reneges on every arrangement he ever makes with me. I need fixed dates with the girls. I need fixed locations. I need fixed times, structure, plan. I know I feel sorry for him but I don't know why, because he doesn't have any empathy or respect for me, or what I do for our girls as a mother? How could I have even contemplated having another dinner with him when he asked me again?

I amaze myself, I truly do. Just remind myself how I felt when he left me in Palma, on that last morning having flown there to see him for the night. The day when I eventually came to the sad revelation that I would ever wake up with him again.

I need to listen to people who know me, as I have already proved to myself that I am not always a good judge of what is best for me—they are far more objective and always will be. Anyway, Trouble lover is in the country and I won't be see him tonight. I wish he were mine. He is the kind of guy I need—hard working, ambitious, funny, handsome, and sociable—enough of that... Maybe I'll see him tomorrow? I've got a lot of work to do now. Need to set up a company account, new business cards and update my website. Keep going, keep going, keep going.

Jules leaves on Friday back to Barbados—I have only seen her three times this trip, so sickening she lives so far away.

At home 10 pm surrounded by boxes, absolutely shattered. Picked up girls. Put a big line around this page, as I have to remember today. So here I am, moving on Friday, starting work on the hotel. Go to the cinema to see the movie 'Sentimental.' Keep focused.

Who knows where I'll be in a year. I will miss my bath—I've always been big on baths—free standing only.

Can't wait to start afresh on the new house—set up my desk work and get on—everything else will fall in place. Lay down my giant sheepskin rug. About time I dry-cleaned it!! Hang curtains, nest. Daisy was cuddled up to me earlier and as she put her hand over my chest she asked if I was wearing a bra as I am so boney—I am extraordinarily thin at the moment—in fact I will go one step further, I look really crap tonight—my face looks very drawn and very old—I really need to stop smoking too!

Olivier	hard. I miss you. I miss
Got so much I'd like to talk to you about. I wouldn't know where to start. I miss you wherever I am. Whatever I do. I don't think I will ever heal, even in 10 years time. It's very	your beauty.... Forgive me for all I have done and for saying goodbye forever now. xxx
Options Reply Open	Options Reply Open

SEPTEMBER 20TH, 2006

Everything is OK now. I'm lying in bed feeling quite satisfied for once. I'm feeling a bit more confident too. The girls are on great form. Trouble's back in town. Raphael called a couple of times too leaving messages and then called again this morning, so I booked my flight to fly out for his birthday party in Ibiza this weekend when Tom has the girls. No doubt that will be interesting. I've been dying to go back there for ages now.

Work has at long last started on the hotel, house is coming together and I'm online after 400 hours on hold with B FUCKING T (our equivalent to AT&T).

Need a bigger bed.

Need a bigger memory in my phone for the obscene amount of texts I'm getting left right and center. It's nice to feel wanted, even if I do choose to be alone.

I ended up letting Trouble in again last night. I think I get him wrong in lots of ways. We had a really long chat before we snuggled up in bed last night, good to talk, even if it is always about his issues and not mine before he crept out before I got the girls up for school. The girls know nothing about him; they have never met him nor will they. Anyway, lovely, spoilt, sexy, arrogant and mildly dull Raphael this weekend, what will that bring, I wonder? Olivier is supposedly taking me out for dinner next week. What the hell will that feel like?

I feel pretty for the first time in ages, not just critical of myself. Making more friends than I've done in a long time, and receiving more invitations than ever which feels good, really good. I'm not missing all the so-called friends that I was so let down and disappointed by when Tom and I split. They obviously weren't what I thought they were to me. I'm so lucky with all the great friends I have all over the world.

I'm so lucky to have such a good family too; even if we are all over the planet we are very much connected. I've met some great people at the school now. All good on the social life. All good on the sex life too (well twice a week is better than nothing!).

Just CRAP on the finances when it doesn't matter how hard you work the bloody overheads swallow every penny! Got to keep working, working, working and kicking butt. I've come a long way. Anything is possible if you believe it.

Hang my pictures on the wall; collect my dry-cleaned sheepskin rug and I'll be there.

Girls are really happy with their school, happy with their home.

Woooooow just got back from Ibiza. What a ridiculous weekend!! Met so many fun people. What a fantastic place. LOVE that island. Danced until I could dance no more! Beautiful sunrises and sunsets. Amazing I made it, considering I took the wrong turning on M25 in the pelting rain on the way to Gatwick, and headed off to Heathrow, running on empty in the car, no time to stop, bumper to bumper traffic, making it to short term car park just as the petrol ran out, with 45 minutes to go before takeoff. Somehow I did it. I made that flight!

Swung into Palma en route and had a couple of Mojitos at Puro beach on the water and four hours later, having been to Raphael's dull birthday dinner full of posing Italians, found myself dancing on a giant bed by the pool at the singer James Blunt's stunning villa, followed by chatting into the night with a very cool guy called Bruce Parry.

He was doing a series of documentaries for the BBC following tribes around the world, going to places no foreigner had been. It was fascinating listening to his adventures. He couldn't believe that I had in fact been to Peru and done the Ayahuasca, which was one of the few experiences he had yet to do. That made me laugh.

I heard the sad news that Tom's Granny Josephine had died when I was sitting on the beach with Bruce the following day. I sat there and cried. I loved her so much. She was by far the coolest member of Tom's family and like my own grandmother, as I'd lost all my grandparents' years before. I really enjoy old people. I will miss her greatly and our funny chats that she and I will only know about. The thrill of introducing our first baby Daisy to her, I will never forget. I was so proud and happy that she got to meet both my girls and spend lots of good times together before she died. Even after Tom and I had gone our separate ways she never turned her back on me. She never blamed me for it all. She had the wisdom to know it takes two to make or break a marriage.

On the Monday morning Tom didn't take the girls to school. When he dropped the girls off to me, without even turning his face to me, he told me I wasn't welcome at the funeral and that I must not go. It really hurt me as I wanted to be there, but I knew that there was no way he would let me. I decided to buy a selection of tulips to plant with the girls in the garden as our own little memorial for her.

I got a call about the deal that I am trying to do—connecting two big players I know with a property deal. If I pull that one off that is school fees and rent covered for the next 18 months. Fingers crossed.

I'm going to make a big casserole and the three of us will eat the lot. I've got my music playing and Daisy is doing a lovely drawing. Troubles causing trouble. Fight the feeling. Leave it alone.

October 10th, 2006

Binned Trouble. Transpired I was just one of many, according to someone I met who knew him—what an asshole. I sat there in shock in my pj's and couldn't even get dressed. I felt really let down. My divorce is officially done on 21st November! I am nearly there. Five weeks to go and I'll be a single woman. (Officially.)

OCTOBER 18TH, 2006

Willy, my father-in-law, has died too. He died a week ago today. It was probably the night he actually died that I let myself down big time. I was embroiled in homework, cooking, washing, working and was subjected to 20 messages from Tom ranging from simple one word "guilt" to "I love you and I miss you", to the girls "hate living in London and they suffer through your selfishness daily."At that I broke, too tired and too pressurized, not even enough money in my account to buy a pint of milk in the morning until the flat sells.

I shouted at the girls and made them both cry. I've never done that before—it was AWFUL. They went to bed, we made up an hour later then I sat alone to cry my eyes out downstairs.

The next day after school, having beaten myself up for 24 hours with guilt—I sat them down and told them both how sorry I was. Amber told me she had heard me crying—it broke my heart into a million pieces.

I had the phone call in the morning to say that Willy had died. I was devastated even after everything that has happened in recent years—he was still my father-in-law, still my daughter's grandfather. We had shared a decade of great memories together.

I had really wanted to see him before he died. I wanted to tell him that I was sorry for hurting him and I wanted to thank him for so many things he had been to me, so many things he had meant to me. I wanted to tell him how much I loved him. I was not welcome. He didn't want to see me. We would never say goodbye.

I took the girls to Sussex to Tom's family, which was like walking into the lion's den, having to subject myself to his ghastly viper sister once more. Not having to see her was at the top of my list of pros to being divorced. His other sister was totally cool and lived in Oz, so it was nice to see her and her lovely husband briefly at least. According to Viper, I wasn't allowed to show my sorrow. I didn't have a right apparently. How dare I cry?

Friday 13th—what a day to remember. Now I am just faced with do I or don't I go to the funeral, we will see. Masses to consider. I will do what I feel is right and not be bullied into anything.

OCTOBER 31ST, 2006

Jesus what a week, it feels like a month. Had my boobs done on Monday, the third, last, and free attempt to lift the effects of breast-feeding two hungry babies and prevent them from drooping around my tummy. (I hated my boobs so much I never wanted anyone to look at them.)

Tuesday I got up with all my bandages and spend half an hour trying to dress myself to drive to my father-in-law's funeral that I am not at all welcome at. My parents came to support me and ironically we met outside the church that Tom and I had got married in before we went together to the service for Willy.

No one knew I was coming and I snuck in at the back at the last moment to watch the service, being looked at like I was a leper. I didn't care. I held my head high. I was there to show my respect and to say goodbye to a man I loved for many years. My babies were singing in front of hundreds of people. I wanted to be there, not just for them, but I also knew in my heart that even though Tom had told me not to come, part of him wanted me there and I was right. He sent me a lovely message later that day thanking me. One of the things he loved about me was my strength and he knew I would be there regardless of anyone.

Wednesday—I suffer the consequences big time of a full day of funerals and driving for

3hours when I should be on my back watching daytime telly for the first time, whilst I give my body at least 48 sodding hours to heal slightly after my op! Bruised and floored.

Thursday—wake up.

Friday—absorb events and try to do some paper work and invoicing.

Girls are returned to me on Sunday, both ill—no sleep on Sunday night. On the phone to hospital. Scarlet fever scare. Daisy got a bad infection and I'm too shattered to write really.

To top it all I have now got a bad cold. Beautiful.

November 9th, 2006

Amber was in hospital for three days. She had an allergic reaction to something she ate at the funeral. Her eyes swelled up like tennis balls and her neck like Tyson, when we were staying at Ralph and Kristy's. Ambulance would take too long so Kristy and I drove flat out to ER. I lay on the floor by her bed in the same hospital where I gave birth to both her and Daisy, watching the fireworks, holding her hand as she slept, feeling almost like I'd been ironed to the floor. I was so exhausted and depleted. I know I could feel tears rolling down my cheeks as I lay there, yet I didn't even have the energy to blink, let alone wipe them away.

What doesn't kill you makes you stronger?

November 17th, 2006

I've been feeling terrible for the past four days. I've got a ridiculously high temperature and feel incredibly weak. After I got up to take the girls to school I came straight home and went back to bed virtually all day. I just can't stop sleeping. I wish I had someone to put their arms around me and stroke my brow. I'm struggling like mad. Haven't got any food left in the fridge for the girls' tea and I haven't got the strength to go back out. I can barely focus on any homework scenarios.

November 18th, 2006

Those last days were like being in a time warp. JESUS!

Everyone is healthy again!!!!

Tits feeling better, at last.

Two buyers on my flat—HOORAY.

Hotel coming together brilliantly.

Two weeks away from not being married.

Spent the night with Trouble—great. He always wins me back over every time he lets me down. There is something about him that is quite addictive. Maybe I just like to hurt myself?

Read through messages on my phone from Olivier and saw a man I no longer want to be with. He told me when we first met we were like two planets in the sky crossing, he was so right. Trying to believe in myself. Every day I go through the total self-doubt to then feeling I am going to be fine. I know that one thing leads to another, and I am too loved and so are my babies, to ever be alone and deserted.

November 29th, 2006

I didn't get any better. In fact I got very much worse the day I dragged myself up to be there to see the girls performing in their school assembly. I couldn't miss it but I don't really know how I did it now. I remember sitting there in my saved seat next to Ju watching the girls with a big smile on my face, delirious, with a temperature that wouldn't drop, looking down to see sweat dribbling down my cleavage. Nice.

Ju came home with me afterwards and did her best to make me feel OK. I bullshitted that I was fine until she left, then I lay there all day drifting in and out of consciousness, praying surely I would have to start getting better. Ju then dropped the girls home to me and I somehow made it downstairs to make them some food. That evening having got the girls to bed, I was lying in mine sweating so much I could barely think straight.

The doctor came to see me again telling me I needed to get to hospital immediately. I couldn't face the drama of an ambulance so I text my dear friend Tammy who lived close to us.

Outbox

Darling? Where are you?
Would you do me a big
favour and drive me up to
Chelsea and Westminster?
I don't want to go in an
ambulance but I need
proper help now

Options   Reply   Open

Within half an hour I was sitting warping in the waiting room of A and E asking her if she minded popping across the road and grabbing me a bottle of Evian to relieve my dry throat. I sat there alone with everyone in and out of focus when I heard my name called. I got up and disappeared through a curtain into the hands of my saviors, hugging Tammy goodbye.

I was barely still on earth when within seconds four intravenous lines were plunged into my arms, but I recall the pain. I heard all these voices around me loud and distant referring to the state I was in, unable to focus or keep my eyes open but I could sense there were at least six or seven people by my side. Panic stations galore.

 All these angels... Thank god. Please save me. I know I've really fucked up but I'm sorry about everything I've done. I'm sorry for my babies. I'm sorry for my family. I'm even sorry for my ex-husband right now (and that really is hardcore). I know I'm about to die. I can feel myself going and the saddest part is, that I kind of feel relieved about it all.

I knew I was a state of emergency. My temperature was 105 and my blood pressure was plummeting 60/30. I was checking out. I actually theoretically should have been dead.

I was stabilized and waiting on my stretcher for x-rays just as 'Chasing Cars' started playing on the radio, still with two nurses monitoring me. The icing on the cake for me, as that was the song that made me think of Trouble more than anything. We both loved that song. I lay there in a badly lit, dirty, overcrowded corridor with a mask over my face, with more lines into me than the London telephone exchange, not caring about all the bandaged, bleeding people sitting in rows watching me going by like a hearse and I began to howl. I howled like a child.

All I needed was him here. I wanted him here, by my side. To make me feel like I could get through anything, that I would be OK. I just needed him to reassure me that the girls and I would be fine, to say anything to me would have given me hope.

He was on holiday with his on/off girlfriend in Dubai. Was this what being a grownup alone was like? Was this what the result was of a woman who had taken a chance at happiness? Is this what I had ended up becoming? I couldn't even look after myself, let alone two children single handedly. I was, in fact, even useless to myself.

> **Kristy**
>
> You poor baby, don't look at it as déjà vu darling as you have dealt with everything so well and there is only so much even you can take. U have so many mates who love you
>
> Options   Reply   Open

> So much, don't ever forget that. You are in the best hands there now. Sleep well. I will come and see you in the morning
>
> xxxxxxxxxxxxx
>
> Options   Reply   Open

Katie arrived in the morning from the country to help the girls and me.

When my bleary eyes caught hers appearing from behind the screen, I hadn't moved for hours, but had just had enough strength to reach my arms out to her. In over twenty years I'd never seen her shocked before, as she was the type of woman who seemed to take everything in her stride. She was floored when she saw me, so that really shocked me. God, I must look in a right state. Thank god there were no mirrors! She even had tears in her eyes as she held me. Irish women don't do that kind of stuff on a regular basis!

She took charge like a mother for the next week, dealing with my babies, collecting them from school, walking them home, reassuring them about Mummy's health, feeding them, helping with their homework, getting their kit together daily as well as coming to visit me and cheer me up with her company and good food for me. She even made friends with some of the mothers from school I'd never met. She stepped into my shoes heroically. Major crisis times again. My mother Teresa tenfold.

She took the girls home to my father's and came back to London with him the next day. What is it with fathers with always needing them to see you on form as a mother? I could hardly look like I was coping with a plastic mask over my face, unable to hug him with all the tubes onto me from drips. Sorry Dad. Your daughter isn't actually coping that well right now. She isn't capable of making you proud at the moment. The fact that he drove my new car the hour and half back to his house made me happy, as I knew at least he would have enjoyed driving it! That was all that I could be happy about.

I spent ten days and ten nights in a twelve foot squared section in Chelsea and Westminster hospital getting back to a point where I was able to stand on my own two feet again, before being discharged, having done nothing but think about my life, all the mistakes I'd made, all the people I'd hurt and where the hell I was headed next.

And then I bounced back (like I always seem to!) and when I walked into school ten days later, most people didn't even know I'd been to death's door, knocked and come back. I looked fine and put on my biggest smile yet. They probably thought I was globetrotting again, with my über-glamorous lifestyle they all imagined! Only a few more days and the girls would be with Tom for the next two weeks of their holidays, freeing me, so that I didn't need to be responsible for them briefly. I had a date with my best friend, sunshine, a big bed and a lifetime's worth of sleep.

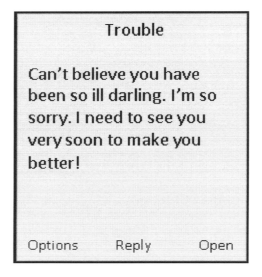

DECEMBER 2ND, 2006

I HAVE DONE IT!!!! I am officially divorced hooray hooray hooray!!!!!

I feel I have crawled a thousand miles, mostly on my knees. Sometimes having my hand held but the hardest times alone. Very, very, very alone. I have climbed a mountain so high—if I had seen it before, I never would have believed I could even start it, let alone climb it and survive. I don't know when or where but I did.

The girls and I sang our hearts out to the entire album to 'Changes' by David Bowie on the way up the A3 back into London, and my heart was filled to the brim with joy.

December 16th 2006

Barbados.

I'm in bed at last. A beautiful nine-foot king, the size of mainland China. A fan slowly turns above my exhausted naked body, and all I can hear are the waves gently breaking on the beach. I'm so happy to be back here in Barbados, even if I'm alone again in a stunning suite made for lovers, not single divorcees. Tom rang me just before I took off and told me he missed me.

"I really miss you darling. I miss seeing all your clothes in the wardrobe. I miss all your baskets in the bathroom full of stuff. I miss the way you make the bed with all your cushions and the way you always make everything look so beautiful. I really miss your smell, darling. I miss everything about you." Eleven hours later those words are still ringing around my head. Why is he saying all this now? Why the hell couldn't he found those words two years ago? What stopped him? God I wish he had. Maybe I wouldn't be here now. Maybe we would all be together as a family. But instead of saying those things to me, all he could say was everything he shouldn't have, to push me further and further away to the point of no return. Maybe I'm just kidding myself wishing lots of things that could never be. All I know is that that call and hearing those words melted my heart, made me cry out loud, and sickened me to the core, compounding just what a lonely road I had chosen. Paradise alone.

I faked smiles. I broke my vows, and I thought I'd love Olivier all my life. I have to remember it's all an illusion. That was then and this is now. Right now I need to sleep, sleep, sleep, recover and try to remember to eat. I look half dead, pale and drawn and can still see the bruises where all the IV's were in my arms—nothing that some Tropicana oil, hot sun and seawater can't sort out. I'm determined to make it to seven stone too.

The best tonic of all will be being with Jules, who knows me better than anyone, who loves me unconditionally, supports me, and doesn't undermine my ever-changing decisions. Better than any type of medication for me! I dropped my phone and it's dead, which is probably a blessing, as I need to detach from the world with all my problems. Everyone will just have to wait and LEAVE ME ALONE! Peace and serenity now please. I'm not going to beat myself up for doing nothing other than reading, sleeping and eating (or being a divorcee!)

I sat under the stars tonight, with all the Christmas decorations adorning the palm trees on the beach, watching the older couples dancing to the band. There was one couple that particularly caught my eye as they danced like they were one person gliding through the moves. They were enchanted by each other. They were staring into each other's eyes, smiling, obviously loving every second they were sharing. It lifted my heart to see them. It made me feel happy inside. I thought to myself whatever they have together—that's what I want.

What I was eternally searching for must exist, because I could see it in them. It reminded me of times when waitresses in bars would come up to Olivier and me and tell us how in love we looked. How precious it was to see. On our third date a lady at the bar said we looked like we'd been together for years. It's funny how wrong one can be.

I don't care that every time I go to the table it gets set for two. I would have enjoyed saying 'bitter' table for one please but I really didn't feel that way. Staff and guests all pretend they aren't all talking about me wondering what my story is being here alone. It's so obvious, but it really doesn't bother me at all. I haven't left here for three days and I'm LOVING every second of being able to be by myself without any responsibilities.

The best therapy. I'm not planning on going anywhere other than walking from my suite down to the perfect, turquoise water, fifteen feet from my terrace and back again.

DECEMBER 17TH, 2006

My parents sent me a card which said *"Anyone who lives within their means, suffers from a serious lack of imagination." —Oscar Wilde;* really made me laugh.

I lay awake last night thinking of writing this book properly—the painstaking task of putting it into some kind of format, imagining if it was worth reading and the thought of other people, who don't know me, would they like to read it? Nearly every day I think about titles, none seems to have hit the nail on the head; I know when it will be right because I know it will make sense. I have learnt to let go and just find answers when they will come naturally in due course. I can already feel my imagination wandering to holding my finished book.

One has to ask the question—where do all the ordinary people live?? Why do I have this extraordinary life when I truly long not to have such drama? Nobody believes me but it's the truth!!

I sent Trouble a kiss and had no response—funny that. He got what he wanted and now I want him, the game is over. He likes me a lot more than what he allows himself to think. I told him that whilst he kissed me and made love to me like he does I am not that likely to be able to give him up. I doubt he will be around over New Year—Cape Town or Miami are on his menu.

DECEMBER 22ND, 2006

Barbados Airport. Delayed. Destination London.

Had a very tearful goodbye with Jules, as always.....life is so unfair sometimes. Why does my best friend in the world live here so far away from me? So annoying. This is my third trip to Barbados in a year. Not a cheap rendezvous, but far better than her living somewhere like Baghdad I suppose. I hate saying goodbye to her, every time we have to.

Am I ready to face the world again and what the festive season has in store for me back in the UK? I'm not sure but I know that I'm a lot stronger than I was a week or so ago when I arrived here, and I look a million times healthier.

So, here I am. Great tan (which never fails to make me feel better!), totally recharged with sleep and even touching seven stone, so back on track, off I trot back to the cold in London. I've learnt a lot in the last week. Needed to clarify life big time.* We laughed with the check-in chick at the Virgin desk as Jules asked her if my future husband could be on the plane?

Let me see, it depends on if I wanted three seats to myself? Forget the future husband, I'm trying to give them up right now (thanks anyway)—give me the seats please! One more hug and I go through to Departures. Once again I hear the familiar words, "Passengers, prepare to board." I've heard that so many times this year. So many flights. So many adventures. My life is nuts. I've got to keep writing or I will start crying again and having a meltdown surrounded by hundreds of holidaymakers is not an option!Sometimes I feel such awe and wonder when I see couples cuddling and kissing. Right now though, I want to stand up and punch the couple next to me they look so smug. That's hardly the Christmas spirit I should feel. I hate Christmas and I hate them for looking so goddamn happy. Go and be happy somewhere else!

I can't believe I've been so ill now for so long. Over a month. Not very impressive for the hard-core, capable, kick-ass single mother I try to think I am!

I find it hard to accept, that the older you get the longer it takes to get over things. That goes for life in general surely? When am I going to wake up to the fact that no one is going to rescue me? No one but me can make my life complete. When I work that out maybe that will mean I will be safe forever. Never be that afraid again.

*When I say clarify, I mean fleeting clarity before the next wave of change.

Last night I had heard the desperately sad song 'Alibi' by David Gray as I'd sat by the pool late in the evening. It took me straight back to a night when Tom and I were going through the worst stage of our divorce—hell on earth. Having been rowing like enemies for days, unable as always to communicate, he had leant into my car window as that played on the radio, held my hand, looked me straight in the eyes and said "I still love you, even if you don't love me." I drove away afterwards, even more confused into that dark night through the woods with the rain pouring down, the wipers on full, crying my eyes out. I could barely see, almost tempted to accelerate. I didn't care then if I crashed and wrapped myself around a tree. It was so incredibly painful even now years later it still feels like yesterday.

Anyway, I'm very happy to have three seats for my night flight tonight, even if it is cattle class, it's fine. Wish someone were at the other end to greet me. I just had a flashback to flying home years ago from Peru with Olivier meeting me at Heathrow. Couldn't sleep for two nights before I flew, I was so excited. Oh how I miss those magical moments and that rush of feelings. Getting that text from him waiting for me at arrivals as I landed saying, "My heart is beating three hundred beats a minute."

Said it all, everything. My heart was on fire and jumped every time I heard from him, spoke to him, saw him, made love to him, and woke up with him. Why the hell did I let go of him? If that wasn't true love, then what is?

Duke, a gay friend, his eyes popping out of his head with excitement as I described Olivier, once said, "Darling, sweetie, he sounds heavenly. You NEVER find everything in a man." I could tell he thought I was mad to have ended it. Maybe I was. I've been so close to calling him over the last few days—to say what? No idea. Hence I've said nothing. What is there to say? "Hope we've done the right thing?" Can't explain ANY of it; Why? Was it because he was too quiet? Too serious? Too jealous? Or just too insecure about me?

Ultimately, sadly he was way too grown up for me. (And he used to turn my music down!) Fairy tales don't always have a happy ending, do they? And I'm certainly no princess.

Let the past go, I say to myself, distracted by a yummy-looking guy with Calvin's poking out of his board shorts smiling at me, offering me a drink over at the bar. To my amusement whilst waiting to board, he had three JD and Cokes in front of him, which he told me, helped his fear of flying. Found that hard to believe with the beanie hat and his messy 'extreme sports' look. He was the epitome of cool, six-foot-plus and very cute indeed. No smoking allowed anywhere, so we sneaked into an empty shop to share a cigarette like schoolchildren behind the bike sheds before we boarded.

Within seconds of the seat belt signs going off, I was just settling down with my music and fourteen miniature pillows when he appeared in all his glory at the end of my aisle.

"I thought you were afraid of flying?" I said, pretending to look surprised...

"Yeah, that was just bollocks," he laughed. He confidently put himself down next to me for the duration and soon it transpired in conversation that Cameron and I were spending Christmas two minutes away from each other and that we both lived in London. We chatted and laughed away the hours, drinking pretty filthy white wine and having a really fun time. To be truthful I don't completely remember how it happened but I kissed him somewhere over the Atlantic. I had no thoughts what so ever of, I shouldn't or I couldn't—I just did purely because I wanted to and I could.

In my whole life I'd never initiated giving a stranger a kiss! Not only was he very handsome but he was very funny too—lethal combination. The whole thing was lovely, wild and reckless. I woke up just before we landed, slightly embarrassed, wrapped in blankets over three seats, with my legs being hugged by the arms of a stranger who was fast asleep. I lay there for several minutes looking at him thinking how much Jules and I would laugh over this one when I told her later. Certainly not husband material thankfully but a great playmate. He went his way for his bags which he'd left in 'his' seat 8 hours before, and I went mine, leaving the plane avoiding eye contact with the rest of my disapproving-looking fellow passengers, who had had to listen to us laughing most of the night. Better than crying babies though, right?

I didn't expect to see him again, but there he was waiting amidst the crowds for me at baggage reclaim. A gentleman as well, offering to get my bags with a huge, beautiful smile that belonged to a gorgeously inappropriate 27-year-old wild child! We traveled by train back to London got our taxis at Victoria and said our goodbyes. Lovely. A perfect leg up for my bruised ego.

My chapel house was freezing as I thought it was a smart thing to do to turn everything off before I left. I changed my mind. I vowed I would never do that again. It's depressing enough to leave the sunshine and beach behind, without making it even harder for yourself when you get back to stepping into a fridge which is empty, and rooms that feel like they've never been heated before. I dived head first into my bed, with my Ugg boots on and pulled the duvet over my head tucking in every gap to read my messages that dear Vodafone had failed to deliver in Barbados. Nothing excited me whatsoever. I faded into sleep thinking how proud I was of myself to have the guts to kiss Cameron and how liberating it was, in a funny divorced, single mother, kind of way! Yay!!

Christmas tomorrow. I HATE all its bringing this year though.

I got up in the morning and drove through the grey to the country, collected the girls and tried as always to be the 'Happy Mummy' for them. I could have won another Oscar for my performance. I wish I had a 'happy' place to be with my babies. A place of our own to be today. A family of our own. Our dogs wagging around us. God I miss them so much. Our dream home in the sun seems like another lifetime ago.

I loathed every second as we walked into friend's homes over flowing with kids, dogs, open fires and presents, though nobody knew. Christmas music and champagne. When I thought it couldn't get any worse, whilst struggling to keep smiling, I got the messages thick and fast of how unhappy the girls must be not to be part of a 'HAPPY FAMILY'.

That I had singlehandedly ruined everything for them and us. (Naturally again, no one would ever forgive me.) Change the record, Tom.

By the end of the day I felt really lost, horribly jet-lagged, out of place and totally inadequate. My carefree trip in the Caribbean, with the journey home, seemed like months ago already and I couldn't wait for it all to be over. How could I ever be capable of creating any fun for them when you can give them it 'all' with your family Mr. Perfect Ex-Husband? Seriously, are you really going to make me pay for this for the rest of my life? Thanks for those messages, and a very Merry Christmas to you too darling.

Cameron rang asking if I wanted to have dinner with him in the country. What a lovely comparison! It was great to hear his voice and his laughter. I think I may have forgotten to mention I have two children over the head-pounding cheap white wine and pretzels.

Trouble called today too. I knew he would. I mean, he's proved time and time again he can't go without me and the reality check I provide for more than two weeks max. He has no one as 'real' as me in his superficial, social climbing, dishonest and insincere life. Reality was a treat to this man. He thinks he's smart but I'm well aware of how much he misses me when he can't see me. Good.

```
+-----------------------------------+
|              Trouble              |
|                                   |
| Been trying to call you.          |
| Where are you and why             |
| aren't you with me?               |
|                                   |
|                                   |
|                                   |
|                                   |
|                                   |
|                                   |
|                                   |
|                                   |
| Options      Reply        Open    |
+-----------------------------------+
```

I didn't answer his repeated calls and thankfully just as I was about to give in to my heart, ignore my head and take the call, he stopped. I listened to his messages where butter wouldn't melt in his mouth, he was so sweet. I deleted them immediately. (If you look at any good Collins English dictionary there is a picture of him under their description of co-dependency.)

I still hate him for sunning himself on the beach with his on/off girlfriend in Dubai when I'm literally dying in Chelsea and Westminster Hospital only two weeks ago. I know he called me as soon as he could escape when he heard, but he is never there for me when I need him, EVER. I know he's not mine but it still doesn't stop me wishing he was, however pathetic that is because he's such a jerk—it's not like he's even drop dead delicious either. Can't work out who's more of an idiot, him or me for seeing him so long. Bastard.

Memo to myself – Buck the fuck up.

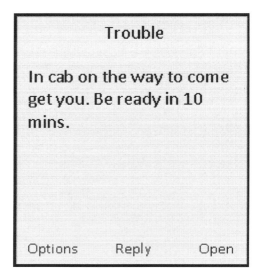

Accept a dinner date from the adorable flight companion who I've been smiling about—why not? Anyone to take my mind off Trouble right now, even though I can't stomach any more forbidden fruit.

What have I learned in the past few weeks? I've learned I can overcome the highest of obstacles. I can still do all the housework, homework, and coffee with a very worried friend, school runs, parent's assembly, full supermarket shop and two loads of washing in one day. My temperature was at 105° but I was still alive when I surrendered to the sweat pouring off me as I was rushed through ER. Excellent.

I've learned I can be very, very wrong about people. I've learned I frequently underestimate my faith in the decisions I've made. I know each one has taken me on a journey. (A lot of hideous ones I would never want to repeat but each one for its own reason). I've learned I can kid myself that I feel fine when Trouble leaves me alone in bed.

I've learnt to let go of trying to find answers, when they will come naturally in due course. I've learned I'm dangerously honest which scares most people, but that's OK too.

What do my babies need and want? The outdoors, the animals, the clean air, the climate, the safe garden to play in under the quiet skies? I'd like no parking wardens and love.

Oh, how I miss wondering around the gardens of Bona Ventura in the cool of the evening with a glass of wine, with the music softly playing, pruning flowers and clipping hedges, twining in the fast-growing bougainvillea. That was always the most satisfying. It was like growing beautiful long hair in a matter of weeks and being able to plait it and make it look stunning.

I adore all my friends in the UK but I can't stay here with this lifestyle purely because of friends. Otherwise this time next year I know I will only be 6 stone, very wrinkled and super stressed out. I want to give the girls back some of what I took away from them.

I want to see them collecting shells and playing in bikini bottoms, welly boots on, pushing the wheelbarrow full of toys around. Healthy, not pale, full of cold and antibiotics playing in a ten-foot square space under a miserable grey sky with the clouds so thick and heavy they almost touch the ground.

Did I actually get around to having a lie-in this holiday? Because I feel like I have been run over. Still got such a bad backache, hope that I don't eternally suffer from 'nine and a half week' sex (the results of a ceramic, unforgiving sink) That really would be disappointing.

I'm very happy with our new home. We have a gorgeous little garden with trees and flowers. We have decking and doors that fold all the way back so the garden is an extension. The ground floor is all open-plan with floorboards throughout. Lovely, arched, gothic windows and little turrets. It suits us perfectly and it's five minutes' walk from school.

Fresh start, all is good apart from being totally and utterly skint. Got to work on that big-time when I can stop being a full-time mother too.

All my siblings are together in Japan tonight – I'm heartbreakingly jealous!!!

CAN'T BELIEVE Trouble after all this time has eventually won me over then lost interest. Shit, what an idiot I am—as if I didn't have enough to feel insecure about. How could he? Maybe he didn't know how big my heart was and how much I felt about everything. Maybe we would have spared me if he knew he would hurt me maybe he wouldn't give a shit—I will never know! I know I miss him.

I drove the girls to my parents in Wiltshire and Trouble rang on route. He was 10 minutes away from where I was—once again I couldn't take my mind off him.

Cameron called and asked if I wanted to meet up—forgot to tell him I had two girls—anyway I will probably tell him next week—he made me laugh; a very funny guy.

```
┌─────────────────────────────────┐
│          Cameron                │
│                                 │
│  Would love to see you          │
│  soon? xxx                      │
│                                 │
│                                 │
│                                 │
│                                 │
│                                 │
│  Options      Reply      Open   │
└─────────────────────────────────┘
```

Tan's fading—still not feeling on top form, but I know the end must be in sight. I need to make a lot of changes in the next week. Bin my expensive babysitters—I am giving it six months to make some serious headway and I am going to try as hard as I can to still make the right decisions for the girls and me—no one else. I am going to try and get this book sorted and do something with it—I am on a mission.

Tom told me to my face today he would never ever, ever take any blame for what had happened—the failure of our marriage. Do you think I didn't know that already? If he had taken some responsibility then maybe, just maybe, we would have been able to meet in the middle. But he wanted me to crawl across the desert alone, parched, and make me come to him, whilst flogging me and punishing me on route—forget it, it was never going to happen.

Where the hell is Trouble? I reach a two-week point and then I burst, does that mean I am a mid-thirties desperate ex-housewife?

Had a good week, funny blind date at a dinner party at Paul's with the aging rock star Paul Young. I thought my life was tragic. Went to bed at 11:30 even more negged out having listened to his woes. Really nice guy, but in a very dark place.

Had dinner with Cameron in Sussex—very funny night, dropped the girls off yesterday and spent another night with Cameron, and I stayed the night with him. I slept in his bed— so cozy, wrapped myself around me all night and I LOVED IT. I have to remind myself that I am single and the only way to work out what I want is to experiment!

Thought about him a lot today. Jesus, what am I doing? 27 years old—really? On Wednesday night we slept next to each other, it felt like we had a thousand times before and it felt so nice—sweet, sweet guy and very funny. I didn't want to leave this morning and I'm looking forward to seeing him again already. Told me he would like to have a baby with me, which was very funny (yeah, right—whatever!)

Trouble called and cancelled New Year's Eve with me—I told him to shove it up his ASS!

2007 is off to a good start. January 12th and even though I am seriously tired—I feel good inside. My fortune is on the turn.

I am deeply flattered and my ego has been kicked right up having this lovely, funny, sexy 27-year-old on my mind who texts me all day, every day.

Work is coming right, which is fantastic. I realized what Trouble has done to my confidence—there's a first time for everything. Anyway he is as screwed up as the rest of us put together.

Cameron is so addictive it is ridiculous. He writes such lovely, lovely things that make me laugh out loud, and he is such a sweetheart. Spoke to him in Dubai this morning, think I must be mad to look forward to seeing him again as it feels like such a long time already. CRAZY. I have no idea how it will be when I see him on Monday, whatever happens I am loving all the message banter between us, it brightens my day so well—such a perfect tonic and such a huge contrast to Trouble and a lot better looking too. Work is really coming together—I am definitely going to earn even more bucks this year and really challenge myself with these new jobs.

If I can convince my way into getting a hotel contract, do it and do it well, without even being there full time, and make a success of it, then I can surely do anything? Get my confidence back. Why the hell does everyone think I am so confident, hard and untouchable?

JANUARY 20TH, 2007

Cameron

Had a great time with you
darling. Wish you could
spend more time with me.
You smelt incredible last
night xxxx

Options   Reply   Open

Feeling depressed for the first time in ages tonight. Spent the last 24 hours of my weekend off with Cameron having the nicest time, and now it's ended, I feel as flat as a pancake. He is so appealing in almost every way but I am actually shaking my head writing this, having to remind myself that he can't be my future—I can't fall in love with him, we are at totally different stages in our lives and they are miles and miles apart.

He fascinates me. Why do I seem to attract causalities that need saving, a consistent pattern of behavior? Maybe I need more therapy?! He is so attractive and is an incredible lover too; oh, the youth of today—so dangerous for me. Why is it the 'in thing' to date an older woman? Why is that so fashionable these days? Again another one that is doomed from the start that I will suffer with. The eternal idiot that I seem to be when falling for unsuitable men.

We met last night on the Old Brompton Road at the Oratory restaurant with three of his friends, he looked absolutely beautiful. He told me he was so proud to be with me and I felt exactly the same. We snuck out of the restaurant to share a cigarette and hugged and shared a kiss outside—it was so electric that it was one kiss that I won't ever forget. I hugged him as I was looking up into the stars above us and felt so happy.

He smiles nearly all the time, and laughs more than anyone I have hung out with for as long as I can remember. I could easily fall in love with him. I can't and I won't. I am a mother with two girls and baggage.

He is a wild rolling stone with a lot of places to roll and a lot of people to meet—I am not what he needs and he is not what I need. His house is full of guys and girls in their 20s—I felt sooooo old. A wild house party, with a flow of people in and out, is not my scene anymore, thank god.

He is going away tomorrow to Austria to detox—he drinks way too much, probably takes too many drugs, and has a terrible diet. He needs looking after, but not by me sadly. Kids and Cameron—too hard to imagine. In another lifetime, in another situation; single with no kids maybe. So I won't see him for 10 days now.

As he kissed me goodbye, through my car window tonight, he told me he was really going to miss me and could I keep the night he gets back for dinner free? We'll see how he feels in 10 days time when he gets back. Why am I always attracted to men that I can't have or are sickeningly unsuitable? I found out a lot about him today. He had a lot of demons with sadness from his past. He had a lot going on in there, and that was another reason I found him so attractive—BOLLOCKS!! Stand away from the 27-year-old. I miss him already. Let's see what happens next.

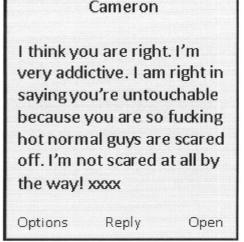

Anyway the good news is—I suppose, I haven't felt low for quite a while; I'll probably feel better tomorrow. It is cold, it's winter, I am alone in bed and it's going to be OK. Desperate for a Viv fix too. Haven't needed one of those for a while either.

JANUARY 22ND, 2007

Didn't need a Viv fix—in fact she didn't even return my call as she's flat out dealing with other peoples issues and it's OK. In fact it is absolutely fine. I am fine—A blip thank God which passed as soon as it arrived. I am in control. I'm really excited about this new project I am getting into; designing a four-floor house from scratch. It will be stunning by the time I have finished with it. I won't be leaving London through lack of work. that's for sure.

Thinking about Cameron and how he is getting on—rice and green tea twice a day and nothing else, sure isn't my idea of a holiday, and I know that he must be really starting to suffer out there. I have a lot of problems, but thankfully that is not one of my issues.

Wonder if he has thought about me? It has been a month since dating him and feels a lot longer. He has taken up a huge amount of my brain in the last few weeks.

Having my hair chopped off tomorrow, fresh start to the New Year, messy and short, far more me—I hate it when hairdressers make me look safe and grown up—I just like to be low maintenance, and anyway I've got enough going on without having to spend any time doing my bloody hair!

I've got my itsy bitsy teenie weenie Diesel denim shorts hanging on the wall tucked into the bottom of a picture frame as a reminder for me every morning and night—I need to shape up in order to get back into them, or rather look half decent in them.

I realize I can go for several days at a time now without needing to call my parents, I am learning to trust my own instincts more. I don't need as much reassurance as I did. I booked a ticket to Menorca today to go next week. Tom and I haven't rowed for at least 10 days which is weird. 2007 has started in a peculiar way in every way really. I quite like it so far. Here's to Tom and I being friends again. Top of my wish list for 2007. Peace Peace. Peace.

JANUARY 24TH, 2007

I am going to design and invent a giant hot water bottle, perfect. Just what I'd like next to me right now. It wouldn't need anything from me (except hot water). It wouldn't give me hard time. It wouldn't hurt me. It wouldn't leave me, and it would be covered in delicious cashmere.

It snowed last night and I was so excited for the girls—I broke my ever-sensible taboo and woke them up in the middle of the night. It was lovely. So beautiful. The three of us snuggled together in our duvets watching the transformation from bleak grey to magical white in the moonlight—a delightfully spontaneous moment and a precious memory. It is bloody freezing in this open-plan chapel though!

The boiler was playing up and the house froze, I froze—reminded me of Bona Ventura when the painfully inadequate generator used to randomly shut down, and I used to be alone with the girls, freezing in the dark for hours and hours in my gilded cage—nightmare. Feels like a lifetime ago now.

January 27th, 2007

Exhausted. Another weekend with the kids, washing and overnight bags, hours and hours in the car. Sunday night bottleneck traffic into London after the weekend at Ralph and Kristy's, with a big week ahead. The boy has gone very quiet—I have no idea what is going on in his head—weird feeling, really.

It has been quite intense and yet now I feel very, very distant mentally. He might be going through a complete reality check, and maybe seeing me again isn't what he needs—and I am big on reality checks.

We had a roast-potato-eating competition today, Tabitha (a good girlfriend) and I had 11 and a half each at a wonderful Sunday lunch at friends' house. Feel very bloated and very tired, but what a fun day; the girls thought it was hilarious!

February 10th, 2007

My weekend off.

Woke up for no reason three times in the night. I feel like I haven't even been to bed. So I watched TV and dozed until midday – heaven, absolute heaven. Drove to the country to have breakfast at Paul's, which by that time, I was so late I was served a beautiful plate of roast pork with all the trimmings. Mission to call into Cameron's parents' house whilst I'm down there, to leave a message that I had been by and would like to know if he is OK.

Find myself sitting at the kitchen table with his parents and him for the next hour—Jesus that was not expected! He said he wanted to cook me dinner tomorrow night in London. Nice. I love a man that can cook.

Trouble woke me up at 2 am ringing from Verbier—I was fast asleep—I didn't respond. What am I to him and what is he to me? God I wish I could work that one out.

FEBRUARY 19TH 2007

What a difference a week can make – Yes, I did dinner at Cameron's. He was really nervous and I found it really uncomfortable for him. He had to drink himself into oblivion before he could relax. Am I really that intimidating? I spent the night with him and that was the last time that I would see him. Sad really. I regret telling him what I thought of him and his lifestyle, as I was in no way passing judgment. I just made him look at himself because I cared.

I said sorry but I still feel bad. We were going to spend Valentine's night together but that was too weird really, and he cancelled last minute, which was a good idea. I ended up spending Valentine's night with Trouble, and then the following night at a dinner party at his too, which was really great fun. I was put next to a 21-year-old Durex model whose naivety to the London scene was really endearing and highly entertaining.

I was aware, for the very first time, of Trouble's discomfort at seeing me chatting with him, which was clearly making him jealous—good! He is human after all? I realized I keep trying to find replacements; this one luckily was a momentary bit of fun at dinner.

I don't want anybody else. Trouble is so deeply complicated—there is so much going on in his head and I am so crap at playing hard to get when it comes to him. He is so fiercely attractive to me—it seems to always be on his terms though.

Haven't slept properly in three weeks and I don't really have any explanation for it—CRAP, is my mind too busy for my brain?

Will someone do me a favor and just hand me a wonderful man who will cook for me once in a while, make love to me a lot, cuddle me even more, and make me laugh? That's all I want—well, actually that's bollocks. I need a lot more than that, I need adventure, I need a challenge, I need fun, I need excitement and I also need stacks of other things—one day maybe...

> ### Trouble
>
> You really confuse me because your madness is so appealingly dangerous to me
>
> Options   Reply   Open

> ### Trouble
>
> You know we must stop seeing each other.
>
> Options   Reply   Open

FEBRUARY 27TH, 2007

I am a bloody freak. I am in love with Trouble, the idiot that I am. He thinks he may still be in love with his ex-girlfriend. Poor guy—doesn't know whether he is coming or going. He is off again. How many times has he done this? Hurts every time he does it even more. I'm lying here, in a sad, pathetic, state wishing it was him that was arriving in the taxi that I can hear outside in the street—BASTARD. Why can't I just give him up—bloody impossible.

MARCH 8TH, 2007

Feeling desperate, have had the worst evening—really tired and really stressed. Didn't finish work on site until 7:30 p.m., rushed home, threw on some clean clothes and spun on my heels back out the door to the dreaded, compulsory, mother's dinner! My best friends Ju and Maxine were the only saving grace in my school life. They had both been so great to the girls and I since we started, lots of fun and always a real pleasure to see. Both married to lovely men too, who are kind to me, and don't view me as a treat for once.

I was so late I rang the restaurant, chatted up the manager and ordered my dinner over the phone, saving me the embarrassment of having to wait when everyone else was eating. When I arrived I was greeted personally by the manager, who bought my dinner to me causing the usual disapproving looks—oh, who cares? My life is busier than theirs, they're probably just jealous, and unlike them I don't have a city boy paying the bills—thank god. What I wasn't prepared for was to be set upon by a praying mantis of a mother, complaining that her daughter had been excluded from Amber's party. After a ten-minute assault, I told her in a very calm voice, with my eyes pricking with tears, that maybe her precious daughter, will have to realize that you can't have everything all the time—an early lesson in life, and as for her mother, although I didn't verbalize it, she should take her frustrations out on her treadmill rather than my fried patience, or just go and either fuck her ugly husband, or fuck off!

Fatal. I had to leave before I cried or let myself down and I didn't even get to eat my chocolate brownie and cream—I went to the bar, paid, was kissed on the hand by the manager who could read my pain, and left quicker than I arrived, with Maxine who dropped me home. She said all the right things and cheered me up en route with a big hug at the end. I would go mad if it wasn't for those two lovely friends.

I am now lying in bed praying for Trouble to rock up and snuggle up to me, show me some sympathy, and let me download. Where the hell is he when I really need him?

I had the most incredible time with him when I flew in from Verbier, having had him on the phone to me the entire time I was working away. When I arrived at his house he was nervously talking non-stop, I just held him and told him to shut up. I put my arms around him for ages—I just lay there feeling my heart on his chest—a very powerful feeling. The closest we had been since we met.

We fell asleep wrapped up in each other. I terrify him, and I know it. He virtually told me that that night and I cried inside. I want so much to believe that he can handle me, I really do but there is this blank part of me that has no answers. I know he felt purely what I felt the other night and it scared him. I am not part of his plan; he doesn't want to fall for me. He never did, I was just a challenge.

He got me in the end and I don't think he was expecting to get me. He is totally unreliable, all over the place, rude, funny, ridiculously sexy, intriguing, childish, game playing, naive, playboy, and country boy—just so appealing to me. He is never going to take me on. When am I just going to face it and realize that I have fallen in love with the wrong man AGAIN! He is actually a lot more fragile than he makes out.

He said last night "All I want is a nice quiet girl with no back chat" we both laughed our heads off! Our sense of humor was parallel. As I write this, he is probably chatting up his next victim, some single, young, unmarried, no kids, sexy little number as he hasn't called me and he is leaving London in the morning. I am on cloud nine when my phone is bleeping and on a sickening low when he does 'switch-off to next week mode'. I've been the other woman for years between him and Olivier, and it is starting to take its toll on me. Think I have got to broaden my horizons, make it easier on myself—not harder. When we walked through Trafalgar Square the other night holding hands it felt so good. He is an idiot. I need a new distraction.

Missing Spain and my easy life (not)—had a siesta this afternoon while the girls were watching a movie and woke up to my ex-husband ranting in my ear. Aahhh, the bliss of just pressing end and going back to sleep.

Went for a massage at 8 p.m.—needed it. My hip feels like it is going to fall off (long story). The Thai girl who walked up and down my back made me feel so much better.

Trouble is sitting next to Lisa Snowdon at a wedding tonight, texting me, feeling very pleased with himself and I'm here eating chocolate and drinking wine. It was nice to be touched, physical contact generally made me feel a lot better. Where is the lovely man in my bed doing that rather than a lovely Thai woman?

The 'twat' landlord has now told me he wants to move back in, now he's seen how lovely I have made it, and so I have found another new home for the girls and I. Trying to get excited about it. It is practical, that's why I am not thrilled yet. It is grown up, it is a bit like the way I felt when my ex-husband ended up nicking my big silver long wheelbase Shogun, and I ended up behind the wheel of his dark green (yes, dark green) BMW Estate at the age of 26—not a good look, or anything that suited me. Well, this house is a responsible mother's house—guess the glass penthouse on the river will have to wait a few years.

MAY 3RD, 2007

Post-Monaco weekend; St. Tropez with my friend Paul whilst girls are with Tom. Got back last night to find my au pair, the only 'dud' in twelve years had let herself, me, the girls and her mother down. She had not only had a wild party with god knows who in our home whilst we were away, but all the beds had been slept in and my clothes worn etc. Made me feel sick. I felt desperate. Should have let her go the minute she arrived, having watched her swap numbers with the cab driver wearing a skirt so short you could almost see her knickers. She had absolutely no respect for our hospitality. Got to bed at 11:30 after having cleaned and stripped the beds and emptied bin bags full of the evidence of her antics. All the liquid and food in the entire house had been eaten and drunk even my favorite vases smashed.

I didn't get to sleep until 3 a.m. I was so wound up, wrote loads of lists and reminded myself as the night grew longer that it's all fine. Look to the future. Get rid of the tarty au pair who needs to go back to school and learn a little respect. Oh how I miss our Tiger. Love how we all keep in contact year after year. All the girls that have worked for me still send birthday cards, Christmas cards etc.

JUNE 14TH, 2007

I got married ten years ago today. Happy anniversary.

SEPTEMBER 18TH, 2007

I've realized I always take to my favorite place in the world when I feel vulnerable and the girls are away. My bed. I wrap myself up in too many clothes, socks with my Ugg boots and wrap myself up into a cocoon, along with yummy M&S food, pints of Robinson's orange squash and the remote control and phone. It doesn't get me anywhere at all mentally but it does recharge my batteries, which are constantly flashing. I'm not going back to ER suffering from exhaustion.

I spent three whole days and nights in bed, my spirit broken, in a very dark place when I FINALLY got to the end with Trouble in June. It was his birthday party and I wasn't invited. Eighteen months of seeing him didn't even warrant an invitation, as many of his friends still don't know about me. Nice feeling. He was in such denial that he couldn't even be honest with his closest friends about how much we saw each other. He treated me like shit so many times with his booty calls, turning up on my doorstep late at night with his lost puppy-dog eyes, and I never failed to let him in. Why? Oh why? The eternal question.

Somewhere along the way I'd fallen in love with him or with the idea of another distressed human who needed saving. I'd wanted beautiful Trouble and everything I didn't need came with it, in abundance. A feeling which unless you've been there is SO crap it's impossible to explain. As well as being his endless counsel to the problems in his life for hours upon hours, looking back, in all that time, he'd given me absolutely nothing other than a few laughs and some sex (which I may add, was nothing to write home about). It was the final straw for me to be so rejected. It broke the camel's back; the day had eventually come where I could take no more. Thank god.

I fell headfirst into the worst place I have EVER been. I couldn't see anyone or even take a call, or answer the door. I wanted to drag myself into the street and just lie there. I wanted to pray for someone to arrive, pick me up, rescue me, wrap me in comfort, stroke me, feed me and cuddle me. Just to love me and save me.

```
┌─────────────────────────────────────┐
│                Sally                 │
│                                      │
│  You can do whatever your            │
│  strange, weird and                  │
│  wonderful life throws your          │
│  way and do it well. You are         │
│  smart, beautiful and funny.         │
│  Not many people have all            │
│  that. Love you  x                   │
│                                      │
│  Options      Reply        Open      │
└─────────────────────────────────────┘
```

How I managed to get away without experiencing that feeling before amazed me. I officially had my heart broken, for the first time in my life, at the age of 36! It absolutely killed me. I was right at the very rock bottom, which apparently you have to reach before you come back. (So the good news is it could only get better) I needed desperately to come back from the edge and the deep blackness but I just couldn't.

I remember lying there in a lost mess staring at the ceiling

As I called Ralph in the middle of the night. When he answered I tried to talk but I couldn't get a word out. I just cried down the phone like a child and he just listened. He knew the tough woman I pretended to be to the rest of the world, was completely broken and he had always hated Trouble. Everything had eventually become too much for me to cope with. Being a single mother, working her ass off to support her babies, paying for a life in London, on top of being treated with such disrespect by someone I adored, finished me off.

Full shutdown of all operations commenced. He had never heard me so desperate for the love of a friend who knew me. I truly felt like I had nothing good to hold on to. Every single friend of mine had disliked Trouble from the start. His smarmy falseness, his hugely overinflated ego, and the extended power he seemed to have over me. I had blanked all their opinions and was going to suffer the consequences BIG-TIME, by myself. Nothing could put right what I got wrong, and once again I was the last to learn. Another sickening learning curve.

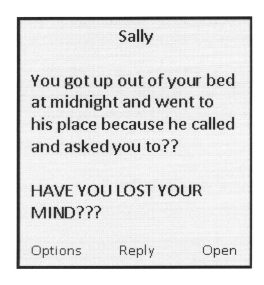

I could hear real frustration and lack of any sympathy in her message. The answer was that yes, I had (but only temporarily.)

No more the fool. I'd unknowingly engaged in a dangerous game and had lost badly. All I could do was lick my wounds and learn from another hard lesson. Payback for those whose hearts I'd broken. Every man who had fallen in love with me had been hurt* and he was the first one who saw me coming and was one step ahead, bastard. Only one thing makes the soul complete and that is love, something he couldn't deliver, even just as a friend to me.

It must have been nearly dawn, as the birds were singing by the time I finally fell asleep. When I woke up with my swollen eyes, the first thing I promised myself—vowed in fact, I

---

*You've ruined my life kind of hurt.

would NEVER see him again. He had taken enough of my time up, when he hadn't actually deserved one second of it. He'd single handedly, crushed any self-esteem I'd regained.

How the hell it happened I would never know. He was my substitute for love. (Or rather my prostitute, who was highly detrimental to my already fragile state of mind.) I'd been dancing with the devil, but what goes around comes around. Karma will catch up with him.

THE END

Darkness always turns into light, and that was the last of Trouble. That was it. I never really looked back after being that unhappy—having had my heart broken in pieces by an idiot. I would never do that again. There's a first time for everything. My sister often said that I always managed to 'come up smelling of roses from whatever shit I got myself into!' I prayed I would this time. There wasn't an inch of me that thought I had a chance of doing that again. But there is nothing worse than giving up when you have everything to gain. Things are constantly changing.

How can I be an apprentice at life at the age of 36? How does that work?

I made the decision, and I made the right choice. My plan in order to ultimately step away from him had to involve leaving the country, as I couldn't be accessible to him. I still wasn't so sure if he turned up I wouldn't let him back in. The girls were on their summer holidays in Spain so I wanted to leave as soon as possible. I accepted an offer to join friends in Portugal, as my first stop on a mission to putting a smile back on my face, as without that, nothing was going to happen. Trouble found out I was there and starting calling saying he was going to fly out for my birthday. He didn't come and I didn't care.

I had a lovely time, just floating in the pool with my shades on, like Dustin Hoffman in the movie 'The Graduate.' I was left alone for one night whilst Ronney, my host, flew back to UK to get his children. Whilst I was sleeping in a separate wing of the main house I heard a noise outside. I sat bolt upright as the door handle to my room was tried! I kept absolutely silent, frozen to the spot with fear. I had no signal on my bloody phone either.

Whoever was out there hadn't gone as I could hear footsteps walking around. Five minutes later which felt like an hour, I had enough signal to call Ronney in London and he called the police. The next twenty minutes of sitting on that bed aged me a decade before I heard a woman calling my name alongside various other voices. I unlocked the door and ran out of that building so fast throwing myself into the arms of a complete stranger—a Portuguese police woman.

They took me into the main house where we put down all the electric door grills we could whilst the officer poured me a drink. They found three cigarette butts outside my door from the intruder, who had been waiting for me to come out thinking he had gone. Dread to think what would have happened if I hadn't had signal at one point, as I would have had to have eventually stepped outside that door. Good start to my vacation.

I went on from Portugal to Menorca, to see the girls then down to St. Tropez where I met a whole new crowd through my friends from Verbier. One minute I'm sitting having drinks on a friend's boat, the next thing I know there is a tender on its way to pick us all up to take us on to a very serious, 195-meter super yacht. Four guests on board and fifty three crew. Oh yeah! It was breathtaking. We enjoyed a dinner on board with the owner and his wife, along with several of their friends who had boats moored nearby. He owned one of the Formula One teams, as well as an empire. Incredible guy. Lovely family.

I was asked if I would like to join the others on the cruise from St. Tropez all the way up to Istanbul. Seriously? YES PLEASE! We would be going up through the Greek isles all the way to the Formula One race. I had always wanted to go to Istanbul and see a race! The girls were going to be with Tom for at least another three weeks so what was stopping me?

I spent the next fourteen nights on board being spoilt rotten with delicious food, copious amounts of the most expensive champagne and cocktails, good company and inspiring scenery. Reading my book. Swimming in the pool. Watching movies. Sleeping really well and thinking a lot about life. It was my time to rebuild my stupid broken heart as well.

I had my own cabin, which had two double beds in with an en suite. Every time I left it, I had my loo roll made to a point, all my cushions arranged and made spotless! It was insane. We eventually arrived as the sun was coming up to the glorious city. We went by helicopter straight to the race, which was brilliant. All of it! Completely surreal.

I met a guy there that owned a dozen properties in Dubai and after having lunch with me and the others, offered to fly me out to redesign at least three of them. How exciting was that? I was genuinely on cloud nine now. My god, Dubai has such a reputation for the luxury of luxury in fabrics and furniture. This would be the most fantastic opportunity to really go wild in the retail therapy sense!

Ronney

Why thank me for being a true friend? That is my pleasure and a true privilege. Life for people like us is striving for perfect intimacy or our perception of it. Always remember

Options   Reply   Open

You have to be strong to be different. Never swim with the shoal. Keep flying high darling and show them what it's like to feel alive. Chin up, tits out. Get on and have fun my dear xx

Options   Reply   Open

SEPTEMBER 29TH, 2007

I don't seem to judge myself as much as I used to. I accept myself more than I ever did before but whether that's a good or bad thing, who knows. My life is flat out. Although it's crazy I'm enjoying the speed of it!

Two weeks ago I had a great interiors job to start in the New Year in Dubai, and now the guy who promised me the work, has basically just asked me if I would sleep with him as well! Really? In his dreams! I'd never be that desperate to pay for life. Overweight, middle-aged Greek men, with breath so bad that you could strip paint with it, somehow doesn't do it for me. Thank you anyway. My summer of freedom and loving had come to an abrupt end! Back to life, back to reality! So that was great news to go into another Christmas with. Deal cancelled. No sodding money due to come in with more bills piling up that I could file away!

Good news is that my rent to that fuckwit of a landlord somehow went through today so the girls and I have a roof over our heads for another month. One big load off my shoulders and I haven't got any school fees due. Not this week anyway!

I do believe in miracles.

I've been accepting dates for once and walking into them with a completely open mind, no agenda, and no preconceived ideas.

Nothing actually other than enjoying exploring myself and the people I seem to attract! People who like taking me out and that I have fun with. Making me feel good about myself. I have many lovely new friends, which make me see the way people perceive me now, for who I am. There's nothing wrong with that.

The dating scene in London is full of women in their late thirties desperate for children, and they may as well go out with that tattooed on their foreheads. Thankfully, I was already ahead on that front, and it showed. My tattoo would read 'no more children required'. I will keep holding out for more, forever if need be. I'd rather be single until I am old and grey; in fact I'd rather die, than ever sell out for less than I want. If I did, that then it would mean that all of this soul searching has been a waste of time, and I can't resign to that EVER! I'm so pathetically unsure of myself so often, but not as much as I used to be. I'm getting better all the time.

My lovely friend Johno, who I met in Ibiza, came to my house and updated my website for me. It looks great and working on the pictures, doing it together reminded me once again I am actually quite talented at what I do—have to keep remembering that. Whilst he was there, I asked him if he would download all my numbers from my phone to my computer. A grownup, responsible thing to do for the first time in my life! He did it, and the very next day, when I left the house to run a friend to the airport, I unknowingly dropped my phone from my pocket outside my house. On my return, a smiling toothless workman who had been digging up the road handed it to me in a hundred pieces. Sweetheart.

Well, apart from needing to buy a new phone—that is called luck and timing: 287 numbers of people I hadn't lost today (but probably only twenty that I wanted or needed to keep).

How does that idiot, turtle-shelled, emotionally retarded Trouble (who still texts me) get into my head? What is wrong with me? Why can't I just except it wasn't my fault or anything I did wrong or that there's anything *that* wrong with me? And why can't he just LEAVE ME ALONE?? I was just monumentally used and made a fool of myself in the process. Come on Cat, get over it. And Trouble, if you could just FUCK OFF forever that would be great!

Putting all my crappy love life aside, I feel quite reckless at the moment. I'm actually really enjoying being single now. This week there's a lot of fun to look forward to but my priority first is to:

Get some sleep.

Earn a lot more cash to pay for the three of us.

Stop smoking.

Stop hating all the things I can't change about my rented house (because it is lovely, it's just not mine).

Stop feeling sorry for myself.

Find a publisher that believes in my scrawl.

Book a holiday to look forward to.

Take pride in how far I have come.

Not worry about the future but have faith in it instead. Relax.

Get fit, and remind myself that I am actually getting older, fast.

Get on.

Be a better sibling, aunty and godmother.

Keep my standards high, reaching for the top where I want to be.

Most importantly, just KEEP GOING! (That's the hardest part.)

Trouble

Guess you won't be speaking to or seeing me anymore then?

Options   Reply   Open

26

Young Aussie looking for hot lady to have dinner with. Any suggestions?

Options   Reply   Open

OCTOBER 19TH, 2007

So when I stood at the checkout of my favorite supermarket in Wandsworth, Southwest London, praying for the all important words 'approved' to show, all I could think about was whether I had time to get home, pack those beautiful gold shoes and that shell-pink backless dress, and make it to the airport in time to catch the night flight to Dubai. Thoroughly irresponsible as I was absolutely penniless, but admitting defeat for the first time in the November rain, let's face it, was never* going to happen! Even with two kids to support, rent to pay, mouths to feed, cars to run, au pairs to pay and sodding parking tickets—I was still going. No hesitation whatsoever. My bank manager would be so proud of me.

Of course I was going to roll the dice again, and cross the fingers and toes that desperately were in need of a pedicure. I always do. If I don't seize any opportunity to follow my crazy destiny right now, there's something not right within. I have a lot of places to go, and a lot more adventures to have yet. I haven't come this far to ever surrender. At least I'm consistent and also the eternal optimist. I'm on a mission to find happiness, remember?!

The girls were due to be with their father this weekend anyway and the sweetheart that I'd been seeing who had left me the ticket would be disappointed if I blew him out.

He was there heading his racing team, who were driving obscenely fast cars around a landscape better suited to Lawrence of Arabia. This would be fun. My fondness for him had grown over the time we'd spent together. He was one of a kind. By far the loveliest guy I'd dated since being back in London. A young boy, who had left Australia in search of his destiny, with a great future ahead, which unbeknownst to him was only briefly going to include me, luckily for him!

He not only laughed when I said, 'Please don't buy me flowers—I need my car serviced,' but he did just that, taking care of it the next day for me. I loved that! God, some of us single girls are really impressed by that kind of treatment. He helped me in many ways but mostly by restoring my faith in men. The first person who actually gave and didn't just take advantage, or use me like Trouble had for so long.

*Never ever ever ever.

The girls had spotted a kids' electric car left out on the street that was obviously broken and had been thrown out, so he took it off to his racing car workshop and returned it to the girls, fixed with more bells and whistles (including their names on it) than they could wish for. Properly pimped up! The autumn evenings of sitting after dinner, chatting by the fire together with a bottle of wine, were a breath of fresh air to me. I looked forward to seeing him every night. He was great, funny, hardworking, handsome, very fit, ambitious and above all genuinely caring; a real honey. OK, the catch—he was ten years younger than me, which for all the unspoken reasons, made our future limited. Short lease, not a long lease. We had to simply enjoy the moment and he made me happy inside. My silver, lining the cloud.

I warned him from the start he was doomed. Getting involved with me would ultimately end in tears, so it made it much harder saying our goodnights because it felt so good. The girls were kept in the dark about any romance going on as per usual, as I never wanted them to get attached. They just thought we were good friends; also Daisy would have got hold of the age gap between us, like a terrier with a bone, and not let that one go in a hurry. It had been a long time since I'd been held by anyone, let alone in the arms of someone so special…Anyway I will cross that bridge when I get to it, but the way it was heading it had all the signs of having a pretty painful ending.

Before I knew it I was knocking back two obligatory glasses of champagne at the Oyster Bar Heathrow. I was off again….

No, I don't but sometimes I wish I did!

I watched the runway lights turn to stars and drifted off with a smile on my face. Within hours I awoke to see the sun rise on the Dubai skyline: one huge construction site. A sea of cranes. New beginnings.

Relieved to have slept on the flight as what lay ahead of me was a whirlwind of fast cars, new money and all-night parties. Little did I know then, but I was right about fresh starts—this is where my new career was going to unfold and my immediate financial problems solved at last. Fi flew out to join us on the next flight arriving armed with a magnum of Veuve, and we proceeded to have the most hilarious time. (The fact that I put it in the freezer and it exploded, I try to forget.)

That pile of unopened bills in the hallway at home was temporarily mentally blocked. Along with the voice messages from the bank, which most certainly weren't going to be heard until next week. Something had to give and I was ready for anything. I was tiring of making houses beautiful for arrogant, unappreciative idiots who thought they were big-time, when they were such small fry, had little class or style, and above all who were cheap.

I was either going to get back to doing my own developments, or take a leap of faith and

do something completely diverse.

26

Gagging to see you! Will be there at the airport to meet you. This will be a fun trip! X

Options   Reply   Open

We all had an incredible four days. From hanging in the pits watching the racing at the

track on the outskirts of Dubai, to catching rays on the beach. Topped off with me at the

end of season party in my ridiculous dress (that I had the confidence to wear at last), getting

a good foot massage. It was 4 a.m. on the terrace of a beautiful suite on the Palm and the

topic of discussion was new careers for me. I had to laugh at myself. The masseuse was a

charming French man who, it transpired, ran the whole show that all the teams and drivers

had come to. His brainchild.

I was safe with him as I wasn't his type and he wasn't mine, so no complications there.

I knew I had cemented a job offer when I managed to whisk him and all his entourage

through tough security lines and past the sea of sheiks to the VIP section of Dubai's hottest

nightclub. Yep, I still had what it took! I'd rather not go in than ever have to stand around

queuing. He evidently only dated brunette supermodels under the age of 25, and although übercool, he was way too superficial and in love with himself for me to be interested in him romantically.

I liked Pablo though. He was very charming, dynamic, and he was so passionate about his work too. I always think it says a lot about a person who earns their living from doing what they enjoy the most. We would be good friends and working with him would be a real adventure I'd enjoy.

Sure enough within a couple of weeks of being back in London he invited me to meet up with a bunch of his friends and colleagues to offer me a job TV presenting. It would mean traveling around the world filming on the weekends from the cities that the racing was taking part in, as well as shooting for a magazine they were starting up. Here we go! And it paid really well.

I had to be at the London boat show next week to do my first show reel. Shit! Now I really felt that panic of 'be careful what you wish for in case it comes true.' How was I going to pull that off? Holding my own at a dinner party or telling an elaborate story to a listening audience was one thing, but standing in front of a camera crew, surrounded by the general public watching me, for the first time reading off an auto cue TERRIFIED me!

That morning I was still tossing around in bed with anxiety at 2 a.m., having gone to bed at 10 to be fresh and alert. Fi picked me up with a mini bottle of Veuve to have for Dutch courage en route (brilliant idea), and I looked just the part when I arrived late thanks to rush hour, bedraggled, with soaking wet hair, looking like I'd just had a fight with a bush. Could I have been more pissed off? I'd managed to hail down a James Bond style buggy to get us from the car park to the event, but naturally for the UK, the rain was coming down sideways in the gale-force winds for my first days presenting. Ideal.

```
┌─────────────────────────────┐
│              26             │
│                             │
│  Going to miss you Guapa.   │
│  Have a great time and look │
│  after yourself please.     │
│  Speak to you in a few      │
│  days? XX                   │
│                             │
│                             │
│  Options    Reply     Open  │
└─────────────────────────────┘
```

HEATHROW, CHRISTMAS EVE, 2007.

Destination Bangkok.

9:30 p.m. Oyster Bar closed? So an obligatory vase of white wine at the not-so-satisfactory bar next door reluctantly, alongside a dodgy bunch of tattooed English holidaymakers swigging pints of lager. Yuck.

Delicious healthy food, sleep, detox, tan and hang out poolside with my really good friend Andre (from Menorca) who now lives there four months of the year. Go to my appointment with my amazing dentist, in his state-of-the-art surgery that costs a tenth of the price of Harley Street London and is ten times better. Oh the stresses of being in Thailand. I wonder if they now massage you whilst having your teeth pulled? Brilliant. Just what the doctor ordered. (Although not the bank manager, who would be much happier in the next few months with my new job.)

Big, open blue skies, chicken salads and delicious ice cold chardonnay, high above the mayhem of Bangkok's bustling streets. Very happy to be back here.

Whilst making and receiving calls from around the globe wishing merry Christmases I lay in the heat by the pool enjoying talking to a man across the other side of the world, who happened to be stuck in a snowstorm in Iowa. He was on his own journey of self-discovery, traveling alongside a little known Illinois senator called Barack Obama, who was on more of a mission of a larger scale. His mission was to change the world. Mutual friends had connected Carl and me once more. I had been crazy about him in the summer of '89 (although we were never lovers). He was wild, unpredictable, exciting and creative, with a unique style.

Eighteen years had passed since we last saw each other, and although our worlds couldn't have been more apart right now, I felt a strong desire to learn more about where he'd been all this time. What he'd done with his life since then. I'd always wondered what had happened to him. I also wanted a really good excuse of why he felt it was acceptable to drop me at Earl's Court tube station in London in 1989, never to be seen again. I knew he had a girlfriend arriving from America, so did he end up marrying her instead? Really? She was seriously an 'off the rails nutcase.' Made me look really sane.

We were so deeply engrossed in chat and laughter across the pond that later, after several dropped calls, when my hair was being cut for the first time in months, I failed to see the 'extreme makeover' that the sweet Thai girl was doing, and lost the entire lot! She took feathering to a whole new dimension, and I hated it.

New Year's Eve 2007, 11 p.m.

Time to go home. What a crap time to fly, but it was last-minute and a gift, so I can't complain. Slipping into the back of the sleek, waiting limo, I lowered the window and waved goodbye to Andre with a huge smile on my face. 2008, huh? Will it be GR8?! What had it got in store for me? What was I going back to this time? This week has been so healing. So good for me that I feet a little sad saying farewell, watching all the celebrations going by, as we silently glide through the night on to my next chapter of life.

I now know I'm my only jailkeeper. I'm so happy when I'm away from miserable London, at this time of year, especially here in my favorite country.

'Hotel California' is playing so I ask the driver to turn it up, and turn his mirror away, laughing at myself wriggling around in the back, changing out of my beautiful dress and heels, whilst shaking myself into jeans and t-shirt before arriving at departures.

What are all the 'normal' people doing right now on New Year's Eve? How funny to spend the strike of midnight with my headphones, on standing in Bangkok airport, surrounded by strangers, without one person to bring in the New Year with…

I feel really alive, that's for sure. I wouldn't swap this feeling with anyone.

With my 13-hour flight ahead, 2 melatonin on top of a bottle of Veuve from earlier should help. 26 is there to meet me at the other end. I feel like I'm the victimizer now after three months of seeing him. I really should just call it a day. He's just too lovely and he doesn't deserve this. I know he's trying to play it cool but it's written all over his face and in his voice on the phone.

This wasn't meant to happen. I love being adored by him. If only I was younger or he was a few years older!! Turning away a lover who loves me like this, gives the best back massage around on a regular basis, and who spoils me rotten, I'd have to be clinically insane. Or maybe I'm just growing up. I hope it's the latter. Still, I can't wait to throw my arms around him and spend the next 48 hours at least in bed before I can collect my babies.

I wonder how high the mountain of red bills waiting to greet me on the 1st of January will be. Fantastic. I will walk in, wade through them and up the stairs to my heavenly bed with him in tow (along with ice-cold duty-free champagne of course).

I will remind myself how lovely our home is, that we somehow still have, and appreciate seeing the fine set of wheels still parked outside, that haven't been repossessed yet. Onwards and upwards.

HAPPY NEW YEAR!!

"Change your life, but don't change yourself. You are loved for being you."

The parting words of Andre in Bangkok. I must remember that....

Things to do tomorrow:

Change my life.

January 10th, 2008

My long-lost love called again, this time from a tinpot state called New Hampshire, where he was trying to get to grips in another snowdrift, where his candidate was fighting the racial divide. He was coming to London to bury his beloved 103-year-old grandmother who had brought him up. He wanted to take me for lunch and suggested four different restaurants. When we talked on the phone, rather than the bustling distractions of our usual, daily hectic kitchen scene, I took the phone to lie down in my room in peace. Man, does that guy like to talk! His voice was just the same as I remembered it, lovely. We were constantly interrupting each other, like we were just taking up where we left off 18 years ago, it was so natural. He also made me laugh to the point of almost being embarrassed. After nearly an hour we said our goodbyes and had fixed our lunch date for next week. I realized later, when I put the girls to bed that I'd probably sat there for ages alone in deep thought, thinking about how bizarre seeing him again would be. I was really looking forward to it already. Next week, huh?.....

Carl

I'm so looking forward to seeing you again after all these years! X

Options   Reply   Open

JANUARY 16TH, 2008

Had calls from the production company today saying how well my first show reel went and they were sending my contract tomorrow. They said that what I did in those hours would take any normal presenter ten times as long! I'M NOT COMPLETELY USELESS!!!! To have put myself out there to try something completely new was quite scary for someone who pretends they don't get scared. It paid off and I patted myself on the back, which I rarely can do. This will help ease the pressure of providing for my babies. I couldn't wait to start.

All new people. New team, loads of fun and lots of hard work. I'm at my happiest working as a member of a team. I will have to be very clever about arranging my weekends with Tom months in advance when I'm away working from now on. He will just HAVE to be consistent for once. Failing that, as he never will be, I need to make sure I have our lovely Mira on standby.

January 25th, 2008

Carl and I met for lunch at Scott's in Mayfair, and as I pulled up in the taxi he was standing there waiting outside, wearing the coolest shades I'd seen in years. He could have been posing for a shoot in GQ! OMG. He looked just as handsome and as wonderful as he did all those years ago, in fact even better.

Within two glasses of champagne, I knew I didn't want lunch to ever end. We sat there trying to fill in two decades of our lives (mostly him talking of course) and at one point

I was laughing so much I did actually feel mildly sick for a moment, hiding behind my menu! We had a lot to catch up on…

I had been pretty naive back in 1989, as I had no idea about his problem. I never saw it. I never heard about it, but years later a few random sources told me he had some real issues. He had married that nutcase, who it transpired had the same issues too. That was the love they shared. They had divorced a year later. He had burnt his way through hundreds of thousands of pounds of inheritance and lost at least ten years of his life. After the tales of turning it all around and changing his existence, I was truly impressed. I'm sure it took incredible strength to overcome what he had and survive.

I had one girlfriend who had been AA and she never took anything or drank again and she would go to AA meetings once a week. I thought to myself, he obviously must be stronger than her, because he could still drink and smoke and not need group sessions.

His biggest regret was that he hadn't had children, never married again, but instead had immersed himself in his photography to become one of the most respected in his field. His life story had me transfixed. Incredibly creative, hysterically funny, hot as they come and totally unique. As he told me another tale I lost myself in my own thoughts…We could be a match made in heaven. Why the hell didn't we get together all those years ago? I could have prevented him from going down that sad road, we would have had a dozen kids and spent the last two decades being creative and having an absolute ball.

We reluctantly said goodbye, even though we had already arranged to meet for dinner as tomorrow was way too far away! We then had another lunch and dinner, and then I asked if he would like to come out to the country for the weekend with the girls and me. We were packing up the car outside the house when he arrived in his taxi. I couldn't wait to take him out of town, introduce him to some friends and spend some more time together.

"Is that him?" Amber giggled.

"Look what he's wearing to go to the country!" she said, mocking his cashmere coat and shiny shoes. He didn't look like he could walk through muddy fields in that outfit, more suitable for a New York fashion shoot. Immaculately dressed was an understatement. After they had introduced themselves we headed off down the motorway. Carl spent the entire journey turning around in the front seat, talking to the girls, swapping sweets that he'd brought for them. They loved him teasing me and ganging up on me with them. Plus he liked sweets too.

We arrived at Ralph and Kristy's to a full roast lamb with all the trimmings, alongside roaring fires followed with great after-dinner chats. Whilst being a true Leo lion, lying by the fire, I found myself looking deep into him, only half listening to a tale he was telling Ralph. He looked absolutely lovely. I would catch his eyes smiling at me. I sooo wasn't ready to fall in love. All those feelings of vulnerability. He lived in America; I lived with the girls in London. I was just about to start this exciting new job. How could it happen? How could that ever work? He was tied to the White House and I was tied to the UK for the sake of my girls' relationship with their daddy. Slight contrast there. We slept in the same bed with my back firmly facing him and giggled ourselves to sleep.

When I woke up I thought about 26 and how hurt he would be if he could see me even though I wasn't doing anything wrong. I hated the fact that I was never going to be able to change the outcome between us. It was always going to be only a matter of time before our lease ran out. I took Carl to the station as he had a family lunch back in town. The minute I dropped him off I wanted to be picking him back up. He was leaving to go back to the States in 24 hours and I wouldn't see him for god knows how long. I drove back, to hear Kristy in the kitchen really excitedly saying, "Love, he's bloody gorgeous! What a great guy!" Yes he was, she was right. I felt totally deflated and freaked out by being so sad to say goodbye to someone I hadn't seen for eighteen years, who was now leaving me again! I don't know why I thought we could have left it there.

```
┌─────────────────────────────────┐
│              Carl               │
│                                 │
│  After eighteen years of not    │
│  seeing you I miss you after    │
│    three minutes!!! xxxx        │
│                                 │
│                                 │
│                                 │
│  Options      Reply      Open   │
└─────────────────────────────────┘
```

When I read that it confirmed I HAD to see him again before he flew home. I asked him if he'd like to come to dinner when we were back in London tomorrow night, his last night here.

I rushed up the A3 to the usual bottleneck traffic, unloaded the wagon, washing everything ready for school in the morning, usual Sunday-night organization, girls bathed, tea, homework, hair washed, two steaks prepped with half an hour to go. Time to have a quick soak and make myself look vaguely nice just as the doorbell went. Oh no! I froze in the bathroom, thinking you *cannot* be early, surely? Who is early for a dinner date at home? Daisy rushed to the door and greeted him, saying "Mummy is in the bathroom upstairs with a glass of wine on the loo, putting makeup on." Thanks for that, Daisy! The reality being, yes, I did have a glass of wine, placed on top of the loo seat whilst I was running a bath!

"What's Mummy doing putting makeup on, on a Sunday night? Ashley, you weirdo!" he called up the stairs. I loved the fact he called me by my maiden name, plus I loved the fact that he didn't care that I looked crap, that I wasn't all shiny and pristine.

Dinner, by sheer fluke, was delicious, considering I'd been so distracted by him whilst I was cooking! The girls were angels as we tucked them into bed, then he sat looking through my book ideas on the coffee table, where I thought to myself, "If you still like me after reading that then you really must be my dream man!"

He really liked it, even though he looked quite shocked by some of it, especially the part about penniless suicidal nights in A and E. It confirmed to him that I was reassuringly crazy, that I was in fact exactly the same woman I was all those years ago that he had liked back then, I just happened to have had quite a lot of stuff going on recently! He didn't want to leave but I was ready for bed and called it a night. We talked until midnight; when his taxi came, we hugged, said goodbye and he left. Mmmm, interesting..

That was it. He was at the forefront of my mind from that moment onwards. He called me every few hours once he landed back in DC and then asked if I'd like to fly to NYC to see a show he was doing on Thursday. Thursday? That was in two days' time! Of course I'd love to! I had to go and sit in my car outside my house to be alone to absorb what was happening to me. I don't think I had never felt this way before in my entire life. I had good friends, Marcus and Tabitha, who were in the middle of moving, staying at the house, and I had Mira, who the girls adored, so I jumped at the offer. I'd only be gone for less than 24 hours.

I stood at the check-in at Heathrow and called my father. "Handsome is as handsome does," he said, with a slight tone in his voice of 'he sounds too good to be true.'.Am I really flying to NYC just for the night to see my long lost love again? I was giddy with excitement to be with him again and ignored my father's reservations within seconds.

The flight was so turbulent that I couldn't help the thought at one moment that none of us on board were going to make it across the Atlantic. Drinks were spilling, trolleys were rolling around, and the seat belts had been strapped up for hours as we rode that giant 747 through hell and back. I could see people looking anxiously at each other, holding hands tightly. Strangely I wasn't nervous; I just wrote in my book 'If I die tonight then at least I have re-met the man I wanted to spend my life with—which was a real bonus!"

When I landed I turned my phone on to see what the plan was. The first text I read was a text from Marcus.

Marcus

The girls aren't home,
where are they?

Options   Reply   Open

OH MY GOD. What the hell is going on?? It was 10:30 at night and whilst I was flying to the USA my girls weren't home? I started sweating with panic so fast I nearly passed out as I tried to push past all the passengers to rush off the plane. Dear god, what has happened? I was in such a state I couldn't even press the buttons on the handset, remember the codes or even breathe. My phone rang almost immediately; it was Carl. "Darling it's OK! The girls are fine. Mira lost the house key so she took the girls home to her house. They are all fine, happy, fed and fast asleep. There is a car waiting for you outside, you will be with me in thirty minutes. A drink awaits you, along with a well-deserved hug too! Everything is fine I promise you."

I cried openly with him on the line. It was all too much for me to absorb. The sheer excitement of flying to see him here in NYC for what could be the hottest date of my life, just for the night, to land to the worst possible news imaginable, rendered me totally numb. The car sped through the streets of NYC to take me to Soho House where my butler greeted me. Nice start.

"Can I get you anything?" this cool, slicked-haired New Yorker offered.

"Yes please, Marlboro Lights! My daughters have been lost and found within four minutes but it has actually aged me thirty years," I managed to smile.

He opened the heavy metal door to the room and off he went to fetch me my crutch. As the door swung open I stood back looking at what seemed to be arrows on the floor starting from the door? They were arrows! Paper arrows leading a trail across one of the most stunning hotel suite I had ever seen in my life. They led to two ice buckets, one with champagne and one with white wine! I loved it! That was the most romantic start to a date I had ever had! "Welcome to NYC, Ashley. Come on in. So pleased you made it," read the handwritten note.

There was wild music playing from all angles as I stood there turning in circles looking around the room at the enormous egg-shaped free standing bath, the giant eight-foot sleigh bed with the glass bathroom heaving with delicious smells of oils, creams and soft cottons, as I sipped on the ice-cold glass of chardonnay.

High up looking out over the city I couldn't work out if I was dreaming. All the emotions of the last hour and a half had me reeling as to what was real and what was not, in my jet-lagged, overexcited brain. I rang Mira again, who was relieved to hear I wasn't livid with her when she told me that they had all been to the park, gone to a cafe for tea, had had a lovely time and that the girls had loved the adventure. Great! I gave her the hotel number and turned my phone off. I knew with the delays I'd missed his show, so I had no idea when he would be back.

I undressed as I ran the biggest, deepest, loveliest bath I had ever had (and that takes some beating) which I was about to climb into; enjoying the dreamy designs of the room, I wondered when he'd arrive. I didn't want to be caught naked on our first date. Not a good look. Just as I was about to lock the door he burst in, at which point I turned and ran to him like a child throwing myself into his arms in my birthday suit! Shit happens. I was so happy to see him I could barely contain myself.

We had the most wonderful dinner in the restaurant and sat up talking, cuddling and laughing until the early hours when I eventually fell asleep, only to be woken to see him showered, dressed, and about to leave again for the airport to rejoin the Obama ride. Where did the time go? I'd flown all the way to America for dinner and it had been and gone already? It was 6 a.m. and he was on the road again, this time back to the Midwest where, by all accounts according to him, weight loss was not part of the campaign promise. I had three more hours before I flew back to London with the biggest smile on my face.

I think I knew then, I was sure that I wanted to spend the rest of my life with this man. I thought about him nonstop the entire trip back home. There was also something intriguingly mysterious about him as well, that I couldn't put my finger on.

26 had called several times and I didn't pick up. I didn't know what to say or how to say it. I guessed in the puzzled tone of his voice when I told him I wasn't around and that I was going to NYC that he knew something was up. The same guy from America who I had spent an innocent four days with last weekend, then I'm in NYC three days later? Really? I had to tell him and I wasn't looking forward to it at all.

He came straight around after dinner when the girls were in bed and greeted me with his big grin at the door, with a bottle of my favorite wine in his hands. I sunk with guilt at the inevitable conversation we were about to have as we took a seat by the fire together. I delayed it as long as I could before I laid it on the line. We were no more. There was no more us. Our time had run out.

He sat there listening to me trying to explain, looking into the flames, nodding like he understood. There was nothing he could say really. It broke my heart hurting him like that. One minute everything was great between us, the next a 'friend' from the past arrives in London, I don't see him for days, then I disappear off to NYC, only to come back to say it's all over. None of it was planned like this. There was never going to be an easy, painless end to us. I wasn't allowed to love him in 'that' way; hence I had always held back any type of commitment.

When he left soon after with his head hung low, I took deep a breath knowing full well how much I was going to miss him being in my life.

He had become one of my best friends, bringing me so much happiness over the past few months and on top of that, the fact that I seriously fancied the pants off him would make it even more confusing. It took me hours to get to sleep that night, couldn't stop thinking about Carl. What was going to happen there, who, and what had I just shut another door on and why? If you are doing the right thing then surely it's supposed to feel right? Hope my destiny knows what it's doing....

26	Beautiful xx
Congratulations. So that's that then. You know how fiercely loyal I am. I'm sure he is a top guy if you're that keen. But if another looser hurts you, I'll break his legs. Speak soon	
Options Reply Open	Options Reply Open

My parents had been away on holiday and I was bursting to share the news. I couldn't tell them over the phone, so I rushed out of London the day they got home. They both sat with bated breath, having no idea what was about to come out of my mouth.

"Whilst you have been away I found my long-lost love that I'm going to grow old with!" I said with tears of excitement creeping down my cheeks. It was one of those priceless, happy moments of big news within a family that are few and far between in enormity.

They were both so thrilled for me. I had eventually found my dream man that I'd been searching for all these years.

Carl came back to see me a week later in London and then the following weekend when the girls were with Tom, I flew to Washington DC for the first time.

Carl

Yesterday was insane. I had four flights drove hundreds of miles and told a presidential candidate at 2am that I had fallen in love and now I'm driving through the night to get

Options   Reply   Open

to an airport for another four hour flight to be there when you arrive. A thousand kisses! xxxxxx

Options   Reply   Open

When I arrived he picked me up from the airport and drove me straight to his ultimate bachelor pad downtown. I walked into his loft hall, lined with his incredible pictures hung on the walls and lit like a gallery. It was stunning. He had such good taste and I love a man with style!

He took me on a whirlwind tour of the nation's capital, after a long lunch at one of his favorite restaurants, The Old Ebbitt.

We drove in the sunshine in his ridiculous muscle car (that I hated) around the White House, the Lincoln and Jefferson Memorials, etc. I'd always imagined Washington to be like other big U.S. cities. This was refreshingly different, in as far as it was so green. I found it amazing that Rock Creek ran through the city itself. I couldn't ever remember being this happy. It seemed he was perfect for me in every way. I was having such a good time with him I didn't want to go home (I just wanted to ship the girls out on the next flight).

One thing I did notice though, was that every time my phone would ring, he would listen with intent, and when a text came through he would ask whom it was from. That was one thing I didn't like. I had had too many years of independence; I would never want to have to answer to anyone when it came to stuff like that, especially as we had only just got together. His phone was always on silent, turned face down.

The other thing that worried me slightly was the fact that he took a sleeping drug I'd never heard of called Ambien, every night religiously. He told me that the whole White House press corps took it, when they were on the road including the WH staff, which I found quite surreal.

```
┌─────────────────────────────┐
│             26              │
│ I really miss lying next to │
│ you. I know the age thing   │
│ was a problem but joking    │
│ aside if you ever want to   │
│ share that gene pool of     │
│ yours I really need an F1   │
│ driver who's the son of a   │
│ real character in life. xxxx│
│                             │
│  Options    Reply    Open   │
└─────────────────────────────┘
```

I froze when I read that. I knew I really had to stop any contact as it was too confusing all round. Carl would FREAK OUT if he saw that 26 had been in contact, even though we all knew where we stood now.

FEBRUARY 8TH, 2008

Tom

Dolly is very ill. She is at the vets. Will keep you posted

Options   Reply   Open

Tom

Dolly has gone.

Options   Reply   Open

It was 6 a.m. when that text came through. Jet-lagged as usual, I had been up and down through the night and happened to look at the time on my phone. Gone? Gone where? What does Tom mean? OMG. She must have died! My brain did not want to take that as real for one second. She was way too precious to me to have lost. I called and spoke to him and the girls, who were inconsolable in their grief. She'd eaten rat poison on the neighbors' farm and it had eaten her insides within 48 hours. We all cried together. I cried all day and all night. More than I think I have at any news of death before. Dolly was my first baby (my delicious, silky, nine-week-old, black Labrador). The most loyal friend to me in the world. End of an era. I was going to miss her terribly.

For the next few weeks Carl would fly over to London every two weeks, or he would fly me out to Washington. We were very much in love and it hurt being apart. My phone was full of messages nonstop. Every time he came to London he would meet more of my friends, and I in return met two couples that he worked with in DC. He was more of a loner than I thought, but seemed happy to meet all my friends.

> Carl
> I want a refund for all
> these missed years my
> darling! What a waste! But
> at least you have two
> fantastic little people to
> show for it all! xxxxxxxxx
>
> Options   Reply   Open

> 26
>
> I'm happy for you babe.
> That lifelong fan goes both
> ways btw. Enjoy the trip
> and I hope there's a ring on
> that finger when you get
> back. You deserve
> happiness. xxxxxx
>
> Options   Reply   Open

MARCH 14, 2008

Heathrow. Destination Paradise.

When Carl, having taken another Ambien on the runway, looked like he was going to propose on a packed plane, I realized it was worrying beyond. He was delirious and it was deeply unattractive seeing him in that state. I had to stop him. I couldn't think of anything worse than accepting his hand in marriage, in those surroundings or in his current condition. Thankfully he soon passed out and then picked a better time to propose when we were in our hut on stilts in the ocean a few days later. Yes, was the answer, on one condition; he would have to get clean. He shouldn't drink spirits either, as after a martini or two he became very jealous, paranoid and aggressive. Another person entirely.

He agreed. I was convinced if he would try his hardest, I would for sure be able to not only free him of the years of toxins, but also make him a happier person within. Obviously, I was convinced that the love of the girls and me would turn all his insecurity into positivity. We would get through it, whatever it took.

We had two weeks in paradise, in the worst weather they had experienced in history. It was absolutely miserable! We had two half-days of sunshine, period. He gave me the most stunning, huge, diamond engagement ring, which he had designed. It was so breathtakingly dazzling that I looked at it every few minutes for days!

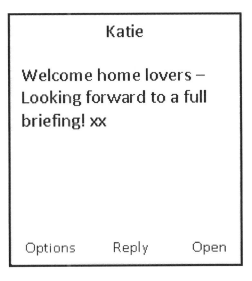

I spent the next few weeks looking at all options for where our new family should live once we were married in August. Carl loved his job and was the top of his game so it seemed a very selfish thing to do expecting him to give that all up to move to the UK.

After an hourlong conversation with my father I suddenly found the courage to make a decision. One that Tom would not be happy with, but one that would make sense to everyone else whose happiness mattered. I had my contract and they would wait for me. The job was mine when I chose to start—period.

I rang Carl.

"Darling, can you talk?"

"Yes baby, I'm just getting on the boss's plane, headed to Tanzania for my whistle stop, five-day, no-sleep tour of east Africa!"

"I have some news for you. Are you sitting down yet?"

"Yes…?"

"We will move to America after all!"

"Are you serious, darling?"

"Yes, baby!"

"One large scotch, please!" he shouted, laughing with delight.

> ### Carl
> Oh my god I can't believe you would make this big move darling. I can't tell you how happy this makes me. I'm truly the happiest man on the planet right now!! Thousand kisses forever!! xxxx
>
> Options   Reply   Open

I promised Tom that it would be a maximum of two years and that he would have them all the holidays as before, but since I had been their main provider, it was actually more my call anyway. The girls were ecstatic at the prospect of living in the USA for a while and settling into our new family life together, the four of us.

Over the course of the following few weeks, we found the best school for the girls and a beautiful house, with a park-size garden, twenty minutes from the White House, in an area called North Chevy Chase. It all looked picture-postcard perfect. We would create a wonderful family and live happy ever after. At last! The girls would have a wonderful new stepfather that would love them, protect them, and cherish them with me. I was already preparing to try for a baby as soon as we were married; in fact I couldn't wait to give Carl a child to make his life complete, as that was all he wished for and the greatest gift I could give him.

I know we had only re-met seven months ago, but I was sure I wanted to love him for the rest of my life by the time I left NYC that day back in January.

We planned the wedding for August 9th.

We started getting ready for the big day. Flights were booked for the four of us for the 12th of August to start our new life in the USA. Girls start their new school on 28th August.

The girls go to Spain for their usual holidays with their Daddy. I hand the passports over on the promise that I will have them returned. I allow Tom to have Mira for the first time ever. Big mistake. On the return from working for him in Spain for two weeks, she is held in customs for two days, and then gets deported from London back to Mexico. He never paid her for her two weeks of work, so she leaves penniless as well. Very sad day. The girls were devastated.

I have my hen weekend and my birthday in Barcelona Hotel Arts with my best girlfriends. The most fantastic few days with the girls I love the most.

26 sends a bottle of champagne to the table wishing me a Happy Birthday from London. OMG. He's sooo lovely. After everything I have done to him, he still adores me. He has to be insane, rather than me, after all!

We arrive in London four days before we get married. Later that day I walk into our hotel room to see Carl, sitting in silence looking like he's seen a ghost. What's happened? Tom has been on the phone ranting at him for past hour, giving him ultimatums and conditions. We have to go to court in 48 hours' time? Tom's bitch lawyer is nonstop emailing me saying I don't have a prayer of getting the girls' passports to leave for the USA.

"You really don't stand a chance," she said. "Who do you think you are? This judge is booked months in advance. I suggest you cancel your flights. You do not have permission to leave. You will be breaking the law, abducting your children under The Hague Convention, so I have contacted Immigration. You won't be going anywhere."

Tom will not give me the passports unless I agreed to five pages of terms including paying for his flights to the USA three times a year. I don't sleep a wink, only to find myself throwing up out of the passenger's car door going around Hyde Park Corner the day before what is supposed to be the happiest day of my life.

How could I have been so stupid to trust him with the passports? My father had made me promise I wouldn't. House is waiting. School is waiting. New life is ready for us all to be together at last. Our new family—in America.

AUGUST 8TH, 2008

I know that song so well, from the Coldplay album 'X and Y.'

"What if you should decide, that you don't want me there in your life, it could bend or it could break...that's the risk that you take."

Jesus. Please don't say that. My stomach churned with anxiety. I pray that I'm doing the right thing. How could he send me that today? That's called balls, I guess. He must really love me. Wonder if he could turn up when the priest asks if there is anyone that has reason for us not to be married? I hope he realizes that although I love him, he is better off without me full stop. He will meet a girl his age, with no baggage, and marry her to live happily ever after, too.....

AUGUST 9TH, 2008

The next song lyrics that fill my head are the words that I had chosen to have played and sung to Carl at the wedding reception. 'Time,' by Ben's Brother, which symbolized every thing I felt for him.

"A second, a minute, an hour, a day and it's gone.

Little by little it fritters away, try as you may you can never replace it.

A moment of beauty you stumble upon,

As long as you treasure whatever it is, whatever it is could never be wasted.

So if we all turn to dust, better to've loved and lost cos everything has a cost.

So if you're gonna spend time, spend it upon me, spend it up on me.

Just give me your time; I don't want your money.

I'd crawl then I'd walk then I'd run but then I'd stumble and fall

Somewhere between the love and the lust, I tried my best I was maladjusted.

And I'm not saying that I know it all

Maybe I'm a little more self-aware, still get scared but I've learned to trust it.

So when it comes to us, I've weighed up all the odds, I bet that this is love.

So if you're gonna spend time, spend it upon me, spend it up on me.

Just give me your time. Don't take it from me.

I know hard it is, getting it right, at a time like this, so you'd better believe, believe, how right
it could be.

So if you're gonna spend time Spend it upon me Spend it up on me. Just give me your time.."

The girls swoon over their new, perfect stepfather, who devotes a long speech to them both. It was all so believable, so perfect, such a fairy tale, in every sense of the word.

"Please raise your glasses everyone. Today I married the man of my dreams!" I announce to the entire room, filled with my family and friends from all over the world, with the biggest, happiest smile across my face.

"Eighteen years late, but better late than never!"

Who would have ever guessed that the 'man of my dreams' that I was so intoxicatingly in love with would in fact within months transform into the man of my worst, sickening nightmares? That my gallant knight in shining armor would so soon and so severely become my jailor and the heaviest, suffocating anchor around my neck? And that over the weeks and months ahead, we would be dealing with depression, disillusionment, deception, disbelief, disrespect, dishonesty and desertion.

And that the girls who had innocently and trustingly believed in their new happy family, would now see the truth—that their mother, who had thrown all caution to the wind to support her husband in America, was unwittingly 'sleeping with the enemy.'

I had received a call at 7a.m. from a stranger, enlightening me about the man I had just married, and to make matters even more surreal, Carl's boss had recommended me for a reality TV show, which meant putting on the bravest face yet, for millions of viewers, whilst I struggled with how to deal with my own dose of harsh reality....

To be continued in Inbox Full, Part 2—*coming soon.*